First World War
and Army of Occupation
War Diary
France, Belgium and Germany

50 DIVISION
151 Infantry Brigade
Loyal North Lancashire Regiment
1/5th Battalion (Territorial Force)
1 February 1915 - 30 December 1915

WO95/2843/5

The Naval & Military Press Ltd
www.nmarchive.com
Published in association with The National Archives

Published by

The Naval & Military Press Ltd

Unit 10 Ridgewood Industrial Park,

Uckfield, East Sussex,

TN22 5QE England

Tel: +44 (0) 1825 749494

www.naval-military-press.com

www.nmarchive.com

This diary has been reprinted in facsimile from the original. Any imperfections are inevitably reproduced and the quality may fall short of modern type and cartographic standards.

© **Crown Copyright**
Images reproduced by permission of The National Archives, London, England, 2015.

Contents

Document type	Place/Title	Date From	Date To
Heading	WO95/2843/5 5 Bn. Loyal North Lancs Rgt. 1915 Feb-Dec		
Heading	50th Division 151st Infy Bde 5th Bn Loyal Nth Lancs Regt 1915 Feb-Dec 1915 To. 55 Dn 166 Bde.		
Heading	6th Division 16th Infy Bde 1-5th Bn Loy. Nth Lancs Regt Feb-May 1915		
Heading	16th Inf. Bde. 6th Div. Battn. disembarked Havre from England 13.2.15. Battn. Joined 16th Bde. 15.2.15. 1/5th Battn. The Loyal North Lancashire Regiment. February 1915		
War Diary		01/02/1915	28/02/1915
Heading	16th Inf. Bde. 6th Div. 1/5th Battn. The Loyal North Lancashire Regiment. March 1915		
War Diary		01/03/1915	31/03/1915
Heading	16th Inf. Bde. 6th Div. 1/5th Battn. The Loyal North Lancashire Regiment. April 1915		
War Diary		01/04/1915	30/04/1915
Heading	16th Inf. Bde. 6th Div. 1/5th Battn. The Loyal North Lancashire Regiment. May 1915		
War Diary		01/05/1915	31/05/1915
Heading	151st Inf. Bde. 50th Div. Battn. Transferred from 16th Inf. Bde. 6th Div. 11.6.15 1/5th Battn. The Loyal North Lancashire Regiment June 1915		
War Diary		01/06/1915	30/06/1915
Heading	151st Inf. Bde. 50th Div. 1/5th Battn. The Loyal North Lancashire Regiment July 1915		
War Diary	Kemmel	01/07/1915	03/07/1915
War Diary	Locre	04/07/1915	09/07/1915
War Diary	Kemmel	10/07/1915	12/07/1915
War Diary	Near Locre	13/07/1915	16/07/1915
War Diary	Pont De Nieppe	17/07/1915	17/07/1915
War Diary	Armentieres	18/07/1915	31/07/1915
Heading	151st Inf. Bde. 50th Div. 1/5th Battn. The Loyal North Lancashire Regiment. August 1915		
War Diary	Armentieres	01/08/1915	31/08/1915
Heading	151st Inf. Bde. 50th Div. 1/5th Battn. The Loyal North Lancashire Regiment. September 1915		
War Diary	Armentieres	01/09/1915	26/09/1915
War Diary	Houplines	26/09/1915	30/09/1915
Heading	151st Inf. Bde. 50th Div. 1/5th Battn. The Loyal North Lancashire Regiment. October 1915		
War Diary	Trenches C 11c 4.3	01/10/1915	08/10/1915
War Diary	C 11.c 4.3 Trenches	10/10/1915	30/10/1915
Heading	151st Inf. Bde. 50th Div. 1/5th Battn. The Loyal North Lancashire Regiment. November 1915		
War Diary	Couplines	01/11/1915	03/11/1915
War Diary	Trenches C11c 4.3 to c17g 3.2 sheet 36	03/11/1915	10/11/1915
War Diary	Steenwercke Parts of A.9.8.14.15&4. Sheet 36	10/11/1915	30/11/1915

Heading	151st Inf. Bde. 50th Div. Battn. attached to 26th Inf. Bde. 9th Div. 21.12.15. (Note. This Battn. Joined 166th Inf. Bde. (55th Div.) upon formation of latter January 1916) 1/5th Battn. The Loyal North Lancashire Regiment. December 1915		
War Diary	Steenwerck Parts of A,9,8,14,15&4. Sheet 36	01/12/1915	05/12/1915
War Diary	Billets Steenwerck Parts of A. 9,8,14,15 &4. Sheet 36	07/12/1915	30/12/1915

WO 95 2843/5

5 BN. LOYAL NORTH LANCS RGT.

1915 FEB - DEC

50TH DIVISION
151ST INFY BDE

5TH BN LOYAL NTH LANCS REGT

1915 FEB ~~5~~ -DEC 1915

To. 55 DIV 166 BDE

ATTACHED { 6TH DIVISION
16TH INFY BDE

1-5TH BN LOY.NTH LANCS REGT
FEB-MAY 1915

1286

16th Inf.Bde.
6th Div.

Battn. disembarked
Havre from England
13.2.15.

Battn. joined
16th Bde. 15.2.15.

1/5th BATTN. THE LOYAL NORTH LANCASHIRE REGIMENT.

F E B R U A R Y

1 9 1 5

Army Form C. 2118.

WAR DIARY
or
INTELLIGENCE SUMMARY
(Erase heading not required.)

Instructions regarding War Diaries and Intelligence Summaries are contained in F. S. Regs., Part II. and the Staff Manual respectively. Title pages will be prepared in manuscript.

Hour, Date, Place	Summary of Events and Information	Remarks and References to Appendices
1915 Feby 1st	Draft of 50 men from Reserve Battn under Capt. Back, Capt. Snell returned to Blackpool same day	
Feby 2nd	17 men joined B Co on from Reserve Coy having stationed at Southdown. Capt. Pilkington now 2nd in command from Army HQ at Short arm. Lt Cocks & 33 men a gun to take over transport	5/47A.
Feb 3rd	Capt. Mackant B. Mhangz & 50 men sent to Thundersley for duty. 70 Gunners & 32 returned from Musketry-Maneuvr fire — be listing Reserve	

Army Form C. 2118.

WAR DIARY
or
INTELLIGENCE SUMMARY
(Erase heading not required.)

Instructions regarding War Diaries and Intelligence Summaries are contained in F. S. Regs., Part II. and the Staff Manual respectively. Title pages will be prepared in manuscript.

Hour, Date, Place	Summary of Events and Information	Remarks and References to Appendices
Feb 1st	Lt. Smith + 13 men arew transports wagons + horses from — Dieppe. Cars filling to strong 920 men however for first days leave	
Feb 6th	19 Mules received	
Feb 8th	New Masingun trench for Rottenrow began to come	
Feb 9th	Lt Lyman Mastons guns went to Shorton Range 1000 Hickens + 65 men return at 1 pm shortem Lt Coe statin with but	

WAR DIARY
INTELLIGENCE SUMMARY

Hour, Date, Place	Summary of Events and Information	Remarks and References to Appendices
1916. Feb. 10th	Underpinning to be ready to move in 48 hours. Lt. Grimson's machine gun section received from Shoreham.	
Feb 11th	Battalion paraded for inspection by Lord Derby (Hon Col.) who was hindered from being present owing to thick fog. Companies issued with new equipment & short mark VII ammunition. Drums were not inspected owing 11 p.m.	

Army Form C. 2118.

WAR DIARY
or
INTELLIGENCE SUMMARY
(Erase heading not required.)

Instructions regarding War Diaries and Intelligence Summaries are contained in F. S. Regs., Part II. and the Staff Manual respectively. Title pages will be prepared in manuscript.

Hour, Date, Place	Summary of Events and Information	Remarks and References to Appendices
1915. Feb 12"	Battalion under command of Major Hudleston left Felix-stowe at no. 1-30, 9-35, & 11-30 a.m. for disembarkation at 7th of March. 29 Officers 1058 other ranks. Long's much transferred to Southampton on S. Tintoretto. Left at 7pm. Escorted by 8 Destroyers, &c. Officers Lieut. R.A.M.C. attached for duty, vice Napoleon R.A.M.C. Officer proceeding to Hospin. Lieut. H. Mack Bowden to 7. Bowden & J. Being Madam. Col. Lambn. - Potts Yeo. tonite tonite Majors Dickson, Blackmouth, York am. Lieut. Dickinson, Dickinson, Blakeman. 2nd Lts A. Stonehart Ward. Hardy Morrow, Stonewell Walker &c. Capt. Hodges Bathhurst turn with the 	

WAR DIARY
INTELLIGENCE SUMMARY

Army Form C. 2118.

Hour, Date, Place	Summary of Events and Information	Remarks and References to Appendices
1916. Feb. 13th.	Disembarked, Havre, France, 10 a.m. Remained in No. 7 Shed, Pongichery all day. All deficiencies of kit made good. Issue of fur coats to mens. Capt. J. Townsley + Lt. went to Base Hospital. Capt. C.F. Bourchier + 58 other ranks to Base Depôt, Rouen.	
Feb. 14th.	Entrained at Gare des Voyageurs 1.59 p.m. Destination unknown. Capt. Makant + 2 Lts. Whalley + Horner with 126 other ranks up to follow by later train. Officers 2nd class carriage. Men 37 per cattle truck.	

WAR DIARY or INTELLIGENCE SUMMARY

Army Form C. 2118.

Hour, Date, Place	Summary of Events and Information	Remarks and References to Appendices
1916 Feb. 16th	Arrived Staimvick 1-30 p.m. Detrained marched to Amentiers, rain in heavy rain, snow. Roads very bad Battalion billeted in Chapelle Armentieres about one mile from trenches.	
Feb. 16th	16th Bde. 6th Div. 31st Army Corps. Regiments in 16th Brigade Buffs, Leicesters, Shropshires, York Lanc. Bde. Cmdr. Genl. Ingouville-Williams C.B. D.S.O. Div. Cmdr. Maj. Genl. Sir J. Kier K.C.B. Army Corps Cmdr. Lt. Genl. Sir W.P. Pulteney K.C.B. D.S.O. Gen. Off. 16 I. Smith-Dorrien G.C.B. D.S.O. Corps Cmdr.	
Feb. 17th	Inspected by Brigadier Gen. Ingouville-Williams C.B. D.S.O. Issued 12,000 rounds extra ammunition to each Coy 9b. Worthington reported missing (Canadians arrived alarm practised by companies)	

WAR DIARY
or
INTELLIGENCE SUMMARY

(Erase heading not required.)

Army Form C. 2118.

Hour, Date, Place	Summary of Events and Information	Remarks and References to Appendices
1915 Feb. 18th	Received notification from War Office of the promotion of T/Sgt. Kenyon, Thos. Marshall, Ward, Glaister to Sergts. (Gazette. 12/2/15)	
Feb. 19th	Heavy shelling of Rue du Bois	
Feb. 20th	C.O. & Adjt. visited trenches with Brigadier. Battalion inspected by G.O.C. Division, Major General J. Keir K.C.B.	3/4
Feb. 21st	Major Caram in Reserve trenches for instruction. Capt. Lonsvrie rejoined for duty. Dr. Worthington, previously reported missing, rejoined.	
Feb. 22nd	"B" Coy. constructing 25 yds. Range. Capt. Potts, Lt. Watson & Chapman, were attached to Shropshire Light Infantry in trenches, for instruction.	

Army Form C. 2118.

WAR DIARY
INTELLIGENCE SUMMARY
(Erase heading not required.)

Hour, Date, Place	Summary of Events and Information	Remarks and References to Appendices
Feb. 23rd	Capt. Read, Offr. Mallin, rehooked attached to King's Shropshire L. Infy. for instruction in the trenches.	
Feb. 24th	C.O. Adjutant, Machine Gun Officer, went to see Bomb throwing.	
Feb. 25th	"B" Coy. testing rifles. "C" Coy. furnished 100 men in 4 reliefs for work near Desheangues Farm on night 25/26.	
Feb. 26"	Lt. Watson & 1 Platoon working party on Division Machine Gun Range. "D" Coy furnished working party, 200, with Indieps, Desheangues Farm.	

WAR DIARY or INTELLIGENCE SUMMARY

Army Form C. 2118.

Hour, Date, Place	Summary of Events and Information	Remarks and References to Appendices

1915.

Feby 27th

Machine Guns to Blue Factory. "D" Coy. billets were shelled. (Shells going into billets. One shell burst in Coy. Qr Mrs stores, damaging ours). "A" Coy. furnished working party of 200 men Dislangues Farm. 2 men wounded No 2666 Pte J. Howard, 1917 Pte Boardman — slight. Corp. G. J. Bouchin, 21 & 6.O's men of "C" Coy. elected for release work in trenches.

Feb. 28th

Sunday. Divine Service Officers Revolver practice. "B" Coy. furnished working party 200 men, near Dislangues Farm. 3 men were wounded 2051 Pte Leigh — severely. 2913 Pte Bareons D — slight. 2793 Yates J — slight. 6 additional men of "C" Coy. joined Corp. G. J. Bouchin's party.

16th Inf.Bde.
6th Div.

1/5th BATTN. THE LOYAL NORTH LANCASHIRE REGIMENT.

M A R C H

1 9 1 5

Army Form C. 2118.

WAR DIARY
~~INTELLIGENCE SUMMARY~~
(Erase heading not required.)

1/4th Bn. E. Lancs. R.

Instructions regarding War Diaries and Intelligence Summaries are contained in F.S. Regs., Part II. and the Staff Manual respectively. Title pages will be prepared in manuscript.

Hour, Date, Place	Summary of Events and Information	Remarks and references to Appendices
1st March 1915.	Transport inspected by Division Commander. D. Coy. found working party of 200 men near FARM. X. 1330 Pt. Aincough F. wounded in head. Lt. Whalley Sgt. Johnson, + 25 men of C. Coy. volunteered for work during night 1-2 March in fire trenches. (No casualties.)	
2nd March 1915.	Capt. C.J. Boucher + 63 men arrived from Base. Major Haslam, Lt. Grierson on leave. Makant. Sgts. Monaghan, Greathead + Fairbank. These attached to York + Lancs in trenches for 24 hours. Machine Guns to Range at Bisie factory for practice.	Summary for month: 6 go on Mount 15-4; lost see 1st 4th. B's attached to 16th B.de. Officers N.C.O's given instruction in trench work by B's. B's furnished working parties daily. Worked in reserve - relieved trenches for part of night from 12-a-m. Coy K + I L 8
3rd March 1915.	Officers visited R.E. workshops. Heavy shelling of town between the hours of 2.15 + 3.15 P.M. One house in our billeting area completely wrecked 3 civilians - one dangerously - + 2 of our men wounded (2.15 P.M.) Pte. Underwood + 161st F.Coy. W.467.101 (Light) Lt. Whalley relieved Capt. Boucher @ Vauxhall Bridge. 21 men placed at Major Boucher's disposal. L. Cpl. Fred Smith Dorrow was to be present at inspection by Gen. Smith Dorrow at 3 P.M.	
4th March 1915.	A Coy furnished working party of 200 men on defence trenches night of 4/5 March. L/C Kenyon on sick list.	

WAR DIARY or INTELLIGENCE SUMMARY.

(Erase heading not required.)

Army Form C. 2118.

Hour, Date, Place	Summary of Events and Information	Remarks and references to Appendices
5th March 1915.	2/Lt Kenyon admitted to hospital. Capt Shaw, Lt Butterworth, & 2/Lt Richardson reported with 8 N.C.O.'s - Sgts. Kay, Gleaves, The Grice, Bayley, L.Sgt. White, Cpls. Boyes, Duffy & Loughlin, attached to K.O.S.L. in trenches for 24 hours instruction. A Platoon commanders, 8 N.C.O.s & 24 men of C. & D. Coys instructed in bomb throwing by Bat. Machine Gun Officer. B. Coy completed construction of 30 yd. Range for use of Battalion. B. Coy found working party 200 men under Capt Dillington. Reserve trenches. 2 Lt Kenyon to Base S/5.	
6th March 1915.	Capt Markant, Lt Dixon & 2/Lt. Morrison + Marshall Sgts. Wooden O.Sgt. Jackson, Sgts. Grundy & Eulmer, Cpls. Crompton, Nichol & Lewis + Denson attached to O.S.S. for instruction in trenches. C. Coy found working party of 200 men under Capt. Meade for work in Reschel trenches.	

Army Form C. 2118.

WAR DIARY
or
INTELLIGENCE SUMMARY.
(Erase heading not required.)

Instructions regarding War Diaries and Intelligence Summaries are contained in F.S. Regs., Part II. and the Staff Manual respectively. Title pages will be prepared in manuscript.

Hour, Date, Place	Summary of Events and Information	Remarks and references to Appendices
7th March 1915.	Officers revolver practice. Received orders to send one platoon into trenches in Bridoux. No.1 Platoon "A" Coy & 1st Party No.1 & 6 O's &c. went into trenches were attached to R.I.R. Lt. Dixon to remain in trenches for 3 days. Capt. Pilling, Lt. Dickinson & 2/Lt. Thornton also attached for 24 hours to R.I.R. "A" Coy warned for working party at 1.30 a.m. 8th cancelled owing to rain.	
8th March 1915.	"A" Coy bathing parade at Erquinghem 9 a.m. Coys instructed to construct shell proof entrenchments in case of heavy shelling of billets.	
9th March 1915.	Major Hassan, Capt. C.T. Boucher + 2/Lt. K.K. McKenzie to trenches. B. Coy. Bathing Parade at 11 a.m. C. " " " 2. P.M. D. " " " 4. P.M.	
10th March 1915.	Col. Grist + 1 section of "A" Coy. to trenches to take over part of the defense. Others received orders to remain in billets from 2 p.m. to 8 p.m. Report from 1st Army received that 8th Division + Mercut Division had captured 1st line of German trenches at 8.30 a.m. + captured 692 prisoners. Received order at 1.30 p.m. for the Batt. to be ready to turn out at any moment.	

Army Form C. 2118.

WAR DIARY
or
INTELLIGENCE SUMMARY.
(Erase heading not required.)

Instructions regarding War Diaries and Intelligence Summaries are contained in F.S. Regs., Part II. and the Staff Manual respectively. Title pages will be prepared in manuscript.

Hour, Date, Place	Summary of Events and Information	Remarks and references to Appendices
11th March 1915.	Working party 50 men under 2/Lt. Dickinson at DU BIE FARM., at 10 P.m. Another party under 2/Lt. Morrison at 1-15 a.m. Pte. Jackson (N.Coy) wounded.	
12th March 1915.	225 men: 56 per Coy. + 57 from D.Coy.) Bathing Parade, Erquinghem, 4 P.m. 1 party of 20 men under Capt. Dilling carrying 5 wagon loads of R.E. material from MARIE to Breastworks. 50 men under Lt. A. Iredale worked on communication trenches 10 P.M. to 1 a.m.; 50 men under Lt. Butcher 10 1 a.m. to 4 a.m. No 2590 Pte. M. Lemlin wounded	
13th March 1915.	Working party of 20 men under 2/Lt. Whalley carrying R.E. material from Marie to Breastworks. "C"Coy. under Capt. Read working on breastworks 1 a.m. to 4 a.m., night of 13/14th Mar. Casualties:- Killed:- 3065 Pte. J. Fletcher h'd on head. Wounded:- Capt. A.V. Mahant (head) and Died 9.45 a.m. 14.3.15. No. 2434 Pte. Norwood A. wounded R. Thigh. " 2351 " Newton J. " Left arm. " 1647 " Hall " Hand-slight Sgt. Gill returned from party in trenches	

WAR DIARY or INTELLIGENCE SUMMARY.

(Erase heading not required.)

Army Form C. 2118.

Instructions regarding War Diaries and Intelligence Summaries are contained in F.S. Regs., Part II. and the Staff Manual respectively. Title pages will be prepared in manuscript.

Hour, Date, Place	Summary of Events and Information	Remarks and references to Appendices
14th March 1915.	Capt. Markam buried in 17th Field Hospital Cemetery west of ARMENTIERES near ECOLE PROFESSIONAL (ISSAGES) (Age 26 years deceased 3 years.) Pte. Fletcher buried N.W. side of FARM DU BIE which lies on south side ARMENTIERES - LILLE road, about 500 yards from Town Place of CHAPELLE D'ARMENTIERES. 16th Brigade withdrawn from trenches night of 13/14 March. Instruction received at 11.30 p.m. to be ready to entrain on receipt of order. Iron rations to be issued and extra ammunition etc.	
15th March 1915.	At 2.0 a.m. received instructions that the Battalion would not be required to entrain with rest of Brigade. Brigade left, going north, Battalion temporarily transferred to 17th Inf. Bde.	
16th March 1915.	16th Bde. returned. Received instructions that the 16th Bde. would take over line held by 2nd Canadian Brigade. A. & D. Coys. to go into the line on night of 17/18. The officers of these Coys. and the Capt. to be at Chilch at cross roads in Bois Grenier at 6.30 p.m. to be met by Canadian representatives & shown their part of the line.	

Army Form C. 2118.

WAR DIARY
or
INTELLIGENCE SUMMARY.
(Erase heading not required.)

Instructions regarding War Diaries and Intelligence Summaries are contained in F.S. Regs., Part II. and the Staff Manual respectively. Title pages will be prepared in manuscript.

Hour, Date, Place	Summary of Events and Information	Remarks and references to Appendices
17th March 1915.	Order re taking over line occupied by the Canadian Brigade cancelled. The 16th Brigade again took over its old line of defence. Two coys withdrawn. Sgt. Whittaker & Pte. Coleman Mason transferred to 174th Coy RE.	
18th March 1915.	Lt. Watson & 25 men of D Coy working party at DU BIE Farm 26th Inft. Bde. 2/Lt. R.R. Mahant, Sgt. Crosley, + 18 men of A Coy for wiring in trenches.	
19th March 1915.	16th Field Ambulance attached to some 16th Infty. Bde. in place of 17th Field Ambulance. 2/Lt. No O'Donnell's Platoon attached to York Lancs. in trenches for 48 hours. Lt. Ward & 25 men working on communication trench behind DU BIE Farm.	
20th March 1915.	Lt. Entwistle + 25 men working behind DUBIE FARM on communication trench between Parties of 1 Officer + 25 men each from C Coy employed on new communication trench. Lt. Dickinson + 24 wounded. 2/Lt. Mahant (party). 2nd Lt. Guinon. 1 N.C.O. 17 men (Machine Gun) sent to trenches for 24 hours. Received communication from War Office that 2/Sgt. G.S. Farrell was gazetted 2/Lt. 11/3/15.	

WAR DIARY or INTELLIGENCE SUMMARY

Army Form C. 2118.

Hour, Date, Place	Summary of Events and Information	Remarks and references to Appendices
21st March 1915.	Capt. Potter's Coy. took over the DESPLANQUES FARM (Reserve Line) from the Y.L. C. & D. Coys. furnished working parties of 1 Officer + 25 men at a time on the DU BIE communication trench. 2/Lt. Mallett with his Platoon for instruction in trenches, attached to K.S.L.I.	
22nd March 1915.	D. Coy. completed communication trench from DU BIE Farm, during the day, and 1 Coy. after dusk. Parties of 1 Officer & 25 men at a time. 2/Lt. Murdoch hit by spent bullet on left knee whilst playing football. 2/Lt. Jarrett placed i/c Bomb Throwers. Major Carlow, Capt. Shaw, and Capt. Read attended Field General Court Martial for instruction. Received wire of fall of NEAVE HILL. Cheers of men in the trenches when returned to the Town. D. Coy. relieved from Reserve line by York Lancs. Brigadier inspected bomb throwing party at 11.30am.	
23rd March 1915.		

WAR DIARY or INTELLIGENCE SUMMARY

Army Form C. 2118.

Hour, Date, Place	Summary of Events and Information	Remarks and references to Appendices
24th March 1915.	Lt. Fowler, L/Sgt. Busby, Cpl. Ryder & 18 selected men of "C" Coy working in parties of 1 N.C.O. & 6 men, on communication trench between DU BIE farm & the trenches. List of men volunteering for patrol duty to German trenches forwarded to Brigade. Lt. Whaley and one platoon "C" Coy, Lt. Dickinson + 2 men "A" Coy to trenches. The former to relieve Lt. Maddett, the latter to take over zig-zag from Yorkshire Hussars(?). 50 men of D Coy working on bridge trench between DU BIE farm & trenches (in 2 parties.) 1st Party, Capt. Potter & Lt. Richardson. 2nd " Capt. Entwistle & Lt. Watson.	
25th March 1915.	Same parties as yesterday working on communication trench from DU BIE farm to trenches.	
26th March 1915.	D Coy occupied Reserve line of trenches (DESTRAMBEURT FARM.) 10 men of "C" Coy working during night on silent dragon between AU MARIE trenches.	

WAR DIARY
or
INTELLIGENCE SUMMARY.
(Erase heading not required.)

Army Form C. 2118.

Hour, Date, Place	Summary of Events and Information	Remarks and references to Appendices
27th March 1916	3 Officers & 75 men of A Coy. working on communication trench behind DU BIE FARM. 10 men from A. Coy. working during night with silent wagon. Relieved the MARIE trenches. "C" Coy. working in parties of 1 Officer + 25 men on billed cage Vivienne behind DU BIE trenches. 2Lt. Thompson to Casualty Clearing Stn. Bailleul. Baths at Englinghem placed at disposal of Battalion.	
28th March 1916.	2Lt. Munson + 24 men of A Coy. relieved by Lt. A. Entwistle + 24 men of B Coy. 2Lt. Marshall & platoon of C Coy. relieved by 2Lt. Richardson & platoon of D Coy. B Coy. working in parties of 1 Officer + 25 men on bicarge traverse between DU BIE trenches. Buttons sewn on great coats so that they can be hooked back like French great coat in order to give greater freedom when marching	

Army Form C. 2118.

WAR DIARY
or
INTELLIGENCE SUMMARY.
(Erase heading not required.)

Instructions regarding War Diaries and Intelligence Summaries are contained in F.S. Regs., Part II. and the Staff Manual respectively. Title pages will be prepared in manuscript.

Hour, Date, Place	Summary of Events and Information	Remarks and references to Appendices
29th March 1915.	Erected moving target for 30 yds. Range. Nickels Dulac transferred to 28th Heavy Bde. R.A. D Coy furnish during night 10 men to work with ateliers wagon between MARIE trenches. D. Coy. working in parties of 1 Officer + 25 men on birdcage traverse between DU BIE trenches.	
30th March 1915.	A Coy in reserve on DESPLANQUES FARM line 30/31. 1 N.C.O. + 10 men working during night on silent wagon between MARIE + trenches. B.Coy. furnish parties of 1 Officer + 30 men during night on bivouags. Lt. Chapman with his platoon Lieut Butterworth + 25 men relieved D. + B. Coy in trenches.	
31st March 1915.	B. Coy. furnished 50 men - D. Coy 50 men working on breastworks S.W. of LILLE R.D. 100 men of D. Coy. working on N.W. of LILLE R.D. 1 man of D Coy. No 1557 Pte. W. Barrett, wounded in shoulder. (about spot where Capt. Moahant was wounded.) 1 Officer + 30 men of B. Coy. work on silent wagon between MARIE + trenches. C.O. instructed Col. Kooya on surmounting obstacles. "Green envelopes" received.	WRO Sam Capt Ref R adj '1/5 New Cap

3298

16th Inf.Bde.
6th Div.

1/5th BATTN. THE LOYAL NORTH LANCASHIRE REGIMENT.

A P R I L

1 9 1 5

WAR DIARY or INTELLIGENCE SUMMARY

Army Form C. 2118.

Hour, Date, Place	Summary of Events and Information	Remarks and references to Appendices
April 1st 1916.	Line taken over by 1/17 Inf. Bde. A Coy provide working party of 50 during night, working immediately in rear of left Coy of our line. B.Coy furnished 10 men for work on silent wagon at MARIE 7pm & another 10 men at 8-30 pm. 2 Officers + 6 men for work with R.E. Lt. Whitehead rejoined from France. C.O. inspected A + B. Coys in surmounting obstacles.	
April 2nd	B.Coy. furnished 2 parties, one of 10 another of 50 men at MARIE at 7.30 p.m. B.Coy. furnished patrol of 20 men working throughout night, work of traverse immediately behind left Coy. of line. D.Coy. also furnished party to Bank up earth on night side of communication trench from Farm DE LA HALLARIE to stream to provide cover from view.	
April 3rd	A Coy. furnished working party of 200 men to work under R.E. on communication trench left about 11.45 A.D. Drew sandbags to complete to 3 hermen. 30 men of B.Coy. for work with R.E. 1 N.C.O + 12 men of B Coy. to Report to OMS. A.S.L.I. at MARIE	

WAR DIARY
or
INTELLIGENCE SUMMARY.
(Erase heading not required.)

Army Form C. 2118.

Hour, Date, Place	Summary of Events and Information	Remarks and references to Appendices
4th April 1915.	Easter Sunday. At 10.20 p.m. a message received from Brigade to keep the look out for a Zeppelin coming from Calais. No Zeppelin was seen.	
5th April	D Coy. took over left centre section of Left Battalion 10 Kfl. Coy line of trenches. C Coy. furnished fatigue for paths DE LA HALLARIE and X. Major Baalam, Capt. Shaw, Capt. Read attended G.O.M. assembled at 2nd York & Lancs. Hd Qrs. for instruction. Received notification from War Office that No. 2698 2/Cpl. Bradyson gazetted 2/Lt posted to 11th Service Battalion L. N. Lanc. R.	
6th April	Captains Shaw, Read & J. Boucher attended J.G.M. held at York Lancs Hd.Q. for instruction. 2/Lt Brampton proceeded to England. A Coy furnished working parties of 30 to work under R.E. carrying materials to trenches, & 50 men to work on new communication trench. B Coy. Ryden + 12 selected men of C Coy. for work on lahs on left of LILLE RD.	

WAR DIARY or INTELLIGENCE SUMMARY.

(Erase heading not required.)

Army Form C. 2118.

Hour, Date, Place	Summary of Events and Information	Remarks and references to Appendices
7th April 1915.	B. Coy. furnished party of 50 men for work on new communication trench 8.30 p.m. No. 1638 Pte. Baxter W. J. D. Coy. wounded — graze, now cheek, slight — through loop hole.	
8th April.	Machine Gun Detachment to Blue Factory 11 a.m. for instruction by Brigade Machine Gun Officer. A Coy. to trenches. 2 M/guns + 1/2 of Machine Gun team to trenches. D Coy. changed places in trenches with Cape Breton's 2nd Bn. K.A.L.I. Battalion takes over the sector of the trenches called the centre section, consequent on this, the distribution of the 10th Inf. Bde. was adjusted held as follows:— Right section — 1/Buffs on 1/Leicester Rgt. Centre — 2 Coys. 5/Ln. R/. 1/R.I.F. or 2/I.F.L. Left — 3 — 1/R.S.F. on 2/I.F.L. The distribution of the left section is:— 3 Coys. – A & B Platoons – in trenches 1 Platoon — DU BIE FARM. 1 Platoon — DE LA HALLARIE and X FMS.	

WAR DIARY or INTELLIGENCE SUMMARY

Army Form C. 2118.

Hour, Date, Place	Summary of Events and Information	Remarks and references to Appendices
8th April contd	The remaining Coy. H.Q., & 1 or 2 Pls. is in reserve at RED FARM. This company will find one section to be at DESPLANQUES Farm by day. By night this section is included to a platoon. Captains L.R. Shaw & C.J. Baucher attended F.G.C.M. at Ypt. H.Qus.	
9th April	B. Coy. furnished 1 Officer + 30 men to work under R.E. collecting material to trenches. C. Coy. furnished 1 Sgt. + 10 men same duty.	
10th April	B. Coy. relieved D. Coy. in trenches. 1 Platoon 4th Gloucesters attached to A.Coy. in trenches for instruction. Instruction received to train 48 Regt. bomb throwers additional.	
13th April	Received 26 Periscopes from Brigade. D. Coy. furnished working party of 36 men for work with R.E. End men no. 2214 Pte. McCarry J. B. Coy. 1286 ———— Murphy A. B.——— was one man 1/4th Gloucester attached for instruction — wounded in trenches accidentally.	

Army Form C. 2118.

WAR DIARY
or
INTELLIGENCE SUMMARY.
(Erase heading not required.)

Hour, Date, Place	Summary of Events and Information	Remarks and references to Appendices
1915 13th April.	No. 2403 Pte. Rees D Coy. accidentally wounded while practising bomb throwing.	
14th April.	Capt. Reade Coy. relieved Major Haslam's Coy in trenches + 2nd Machine Gun Detachment relieved 1st M. Gun detachment. D. Coy furnished working party of 36 men for R.E.	
15th April.	No. 1455 Pte. Clegg R. "C" Coy. wounded. " 2183 " Hanson W.C. " wounded. A. Coy. furnished 2 reliefs of 1 Officer + 50 men each for work on new communication trench. A. Coy. furnished party of 40 men for R.E.	
16th April.	A. Coy. furnished party of 40 men to work for R.E. also 2 parties of 50 men each for work on new communication trench. Capt. Patten Coy. relieved Capt. Shaw's Coy. in trenches. Received 2 machine guns from N.L.I.	

WAR DIARY or INTELLIGENCE SUMMARY.

(Erase heading not required.)

Army Form C. 2118.

Hour, Date, Place	Summary of Events and Information	Remarks and references to Appendices
1915. April 17th	B. Coy. furnished 50 men for R.E. also 2 reliefs of 50 men each of communication trench to orchard.	
April 18.	A Coy. furnished 2 reliefs of 50 men on new communication trench to orchard. Portion of Coy. right centre, breastworks + parapets slightly damaged, and wire entanglement broken by enemy shelling between 11.30 a.m. & 12 noon. 10 other ranks reinforcements arrived from Base, of whom 9 rejoined from sick + 1 from wounded.	
19th April	B. Coy. furnished party of 48 men to work for R.E. forwarded designs by Capt. O.C. Pilling for bomb throwing scoop + bomb carrying basket. B. Coy. furnished parties of 1 N.C.O. + 6 men for work on new communication trench from stream to orchard.	

WAR DIARY
or
INTELLIGENCE SUMMARY.
(Erase heading not required.)

Army Form C. 2118.

Hour, Date, Place	Summary of Events and Information	Remarks and references to Appendices
20th April 1915.	B. Coy. furnished party of 40 men for work under R.E. Major Cadam's Coy. relieved Capt. Read's Coy. in trenches. A Grierson with 1st M.Gun detachment relieved 2nd South + 2nd M.Gun Detachment in trenches. Handed over 2 limbered G.S. wagons + 8 horses to 2nd London Regt. Slight sniping all day on our line of trenches. Moderate shelling of trenches between 1 pm and 2 pm.	
21st April.	Capt. Pilling attended T.G.Cm. 105 instruction field at Headquarters 2/York + Lancs. Regt.	
22nd April.	C. Coy. furnished party of 40 men for work with R.E. Capt. Maris' Coy. (B) relieved Capt. Potter's Coy. (D) in trenches. The second last platoon of Capt. Potter's Coy. were shelled whilst returning to billets. Four casualties:- No. 1730. Cpl. Tayco. M. "2413. Pte. Holting. "2444. — Mulligan J. "2544. — Butler. K. - slight.	All male chiefs also wounded.

WAR DIARY
or
INTELLIGENCE SUMMARY.
(Erase heading not required.)

Army Form C. 2118.

Hour, Date, Place	Summary of Events and Information	Remarks and references to Appendices
22nd April 1915	German flag placed by enemy half way between our trenches & theirs during night of 22/23.	
23rd Apl.	Cadet officer attached to Battalion for 24 hours in trenches. C. Coy. provided 2 parties of 50 men each filling in box traverses. Received information from Brigade that Germans had attacked line on left of Canadian Division using asphyxiating gases. German flag hauled in at 9.35 pm by No. 1954 Pte. Hoole & No. [?] Pte Parkinson No. 5 Section. Captain Griffiths permitted to retain camera vide H.R.O. No. 6 of 22-4-15.	
24th Apl. 1915.	Between 4 am. 4.30 am. about 12 German shells burst around trenches of left Coy. centre section. Machine Gun equipment allotted to D Coy. 9 am to 11 am. D.o. Design of rifle rest by Capt. Greening sent to Bde. HQrs.	

WAR DIARY or INTELLIGENCE SUMMARY

Army Form C. 2118.

Hour, Date, Place	Summary of Events and Information	Remarks and references to Appendices
April 24th 1916	B. Coy furnished carrying party of 20 men. Brigade night HQrs and two parties each of 1 Officer & 50 men for work on new earthworks behind CHARD FM. Rendered diagram to Brigade Head Qrs. showing suggested formation suitable for an attack by battalion on right of an attack. Between 2 p.m. & 3 p.m. our Artillery shelled German trenches. Germans shelling ours in return. Two men B. Coy killed :- No 2806 Pte. Dilworth W. B—— No 2684 —— Harris W. B—— Another man wounded when on sentry duty :- No 1883 Pte. Shadrach T. B. Coy	
April 26th	Two reliefs of 1 Officer & 50 men each from D. Coy working on earthworks behind CHARD FM. In addition to 20 men at MARIE at 7.45 p.m. carrying R.E. material. One man of A. Coy wounded in the head/scalp when on sentry duty :- No 2452 Pte. Coy L/C M.G. 2/Lt Glaister wounded, right foot.	

WAR DIARY
or
INTELLIGENCE SUMMARY.
(Erase heading not required.)

Army Form C. 2118.

Hour, Date, Place	Summary of Events and Information	Remarks and references to Appendices
1915 April 26.	Received further reports re situation N. of YPRES. D Coy. furnished two parties 30 men + 20 men for work with R.E. 2nd M/gun Detachment relieved 1st M/gun Detachment in trenches about noon. Capt. Read's Coy. relieved Major Haslams Coy in trenches. Relief completed by 1 p.m. No 2199 L/Cpl. Smith B. Coy. wounded through neck whilst in trenches.	
April 27th	A Coy. furnished working party for R.E. Received circular re precaution to be adopted against asphyxiating gases.	
April 28th	Inspection of Officers by Major General Keir Cmdg. 6th Division. Capt. Patters Coy relieved Capt Shaw's Coy in trenches. 7 German shells during relief.	
April 29th	H Coy. furnished party of 30 men for work with R.E. one platoon A Coy. full breastworks on R.E. line both sides of LILLE RD. from dusk until dawn.	

Army Form C. 2118.

WAR DIARY
or
INTELLIGENCE SUMMARY.
(Erase heading not required.)

Hour, Date, Place	Summary of Events and Information	Remarks and references to Appendices
1915. April 30th	A Coy. furnished another Platoon for R.E. Endeavours, as the previous night.	Worsley [?] Captain Brig. Adjutant 5th Bn. L. N. Lancs. Regt.

Instructions regarding War Diaries and Intelligence Summaries are contained in F. S. Regs., Part II. and the Staff Manual respectively. Title pages will be prepared in manuscript.

16th Inf.Bde.
6th Div.

1/5th BATTN. THE LOYAL NORTH LANCASHIRE REGIMENT.

M A Y

1 9 1 5

1/5th L'n Lan. R.

WAR DIARY
or
INTELLIGENCE SUMMARY.
(Erase heading not required.)

Army Form C. 2118.

Hour, Date, Place	Summary of Events and Information	Remarks and references to Appendices
1915 1st May	Capt. G. L. Freeman & Lieut. G. A. Freud returned from leave.	
2nd May	Capt. Hadin returned. Major Boylan Co. attended Divn. H.Q. for instructions. Orders received to move to Chateau Duminants. Bn. commenced at 4.30 p.m. marching by ½ Bns. at intervals. D.Coy - 4pm, C.Coy - 4.30pm, A.Coy - 5pm, Bn H.Q. 5.30pm. Bn arrived in billets in farms near Elverdinghe Chateau by 9pm.	
3rd May	The Battn. stood to arms since 7.30 p.m. last night. Each Company furnished 1 Platoon for work in trenches, & 2 Platoons for work on the road from the Chateau to Boesinghe. A new trench was commenced to be used in case of further retirement. Gas mask respirators for men of age not yet received, but we were able to supply to the extent to equip 1 Coy of men per Battn. A.S.C. left yesterday afternoon. Bn. left DESCHACQUES FARM by Coys 1st B Coy 7.45pm, C.Coy 8pm, D Coy 8.15pm, A Coy 8.30pm, arrived legerd between 10 & the Oyserge about 10pm at Malo. The Oyserge Headquarters Battalion Head	

WAR DIARY
INTELLIGENCE SUMMARY
(Erase heading not required.)

Army Form C. 2118.

Hour, Date, Place	Summary of Events and Information	Remarks and references to Appendices
1915 4th May	Both Rest Coy furnished Working parties and 15 men for work with R.E. also party from Service in reserve trenches to dig out right end of DV 3 (communication trench) & on rear trench to trenches to steam. Fatigues (10 D Coy) and 9 permen from Left Coy for altering & replacing old lines. Capt Thain Coy relieved Capt Bolam Coy in trenches No. shelling during night.	
5th May 1915	Both Rest Coy furnished men. Ten men and 1 N.C.O. of Bomb. Coy in reserve for bombing officer. Bar. standing. Officers No Coy relieved Captain... on N right side the R.	
6 May	Both Rest Coy furnished working parties and 30 men as. Heavy bombardment of Ypres... Approximately 100 shells... to Zonnebeke Ridge 9/5... Officers... A Coy. 8.30... 7.9.1915. No 2 [Lieut] B Coy...	

WAR DIARY or INTELLIGENCE SUMMARY

Army Form C. 2118.

(Erase heading not required.)

Hour, Date, Place	Summary of Events and Information	Remarks and references to Appendices
6th May 1916	Whilst advancing was on all side attacked by the N.C.O. Brown. The attack was successful and rifle strength of fort garrison at time much weakened.	
7th May	Capt. Cotton's Coy furnished Recon: for Reserve Trenches	
8th May	Strength of Coy for digging and work round Coy Coy commenced Capt Pitts Coy furnished Ration for Reinforcements.	
9th May	Capt. Potter's Coy furnished Platoon for Reserve Trenches. Bombardment of German trench stones commenced at 4.30 a.m.	
	No. 1509 8/c 10th R. A. Coy. Killed. Sound at 9 a.m. transport 1.30 pm Bombay. Supply of Retondoo found Guides to Capt Reads Coy. Capt. Read's Coy returned. Major Oakham Coy or caused 2nd M.G. Detachment relieved 20th Dragoonsmount shelf commenced at 4 pm. commen 9.30pm	

WAR DIARY
or
INTELLIGENCE SUMMARY.
(Erase heading not required.)

Army Form C. 2118.

Hour, Date, Place	Summary of Events and Information	Remarks and references to Appendices
1915 May 9th	2.0 A.M. The whole Battalion was mustered and taken to Cour-de-l'eau Trenches on return The following were wounded No. 5099 Pte Quiron } 3rd Bn. 5th S.W. Regt Re. — 1867 Rfn [illegible] — 2371 [illegible] — 8226 Pte [illegible] — 2914 [illegible] [illegible lines] 10 pm No.1595 Pte Morgan J alongwanded — G.S.W. Left forearm Major [illegible] [illegible] proceeded to R.A.M. [illegible] [illegible] returned to company headquarters	
10th May		

WAR DIARY or INTELLIGENCE SUMMARY

Army Form C. 2118.

Hour, Date, Place	Summary of Events and Information	Remarks and references to Appendices
11 May 1915	Major Houlton left to attend Advanced Class of Instruction by Major General Kenyon. No 12713 Pte. Jones to ADep 6 Div. 5302 ... Gardiner II - 1 G.S.W. R. foot. B.O.H received acc. of day.	
12th May	Major Houlton left completing earthworks. Major Howland and Ponwell placing 1 platoon for Reserve Trenches. Reconnaissance in relation to Reserve Hill at front positions previously to engage no. on 28/11/15	
13. May.	Coyt. Officers busy constructing materially. O.M. inspection platoon for Reserve trenches. Major Galaway [?] went to inspect party of R.A.L.J. entrenchments by night. (Cant. Kinjale with him.) Three troopers went on despatch as a team. 500 respirators received from Fort Berry. Major Stitchell went to HQ in trenches.	

WAR DIARY
or
INTELLIGENCE SUMMARY.
(Erase heading not required.)

Army Form C. 2118.

Hour, Date, Place	Summary of Events and Information	Remarks and references to Appendices
1915 14th May	Night passed quietly. Enemy shelled road to our left time after. R. Breh moved to the Brewery. 10.P.M. Relieved B Coy of Wiltshires and took their place.	
15th May	C. Smith member Court of Inquiry on damage to Brielen. K.20 Retaliation actually made, received from Dugout No. 93 also quantity of cotton waste 2.15. 19. 1st Essex 2nd Bn. Bedford Essex Regt. reached to Bday. passed westwards. Capt. Henson Bunn to cotton waste of the reguts of 6th Division who passed on from onions. Submitted sketch map to Brigade 9.15 P.M. R. W. Gun Nov 9th Division. Fortnightly Ek tompo ation & autovisor of same. Movement of enemy in support proceeding south wastewas bye one of our patrols from 9.30 P.M. to 10–16 P.M.	

WAR DIARY
or
INTELLIGENCE SUMMARY.
(Erase heading not required.)

Army Form C. 2118.

Hour, Date, Place	Summary of Events and Information	Remarks and references to Appendices
1915 15th May (cont.)	No. 2425 Pte. Parkinson A. Acoy wounded G.S.W. scalp. Bn. Pte Summers H. D. Coy wounded G.S.W. left foot — self inflicted. Brigade relieved intention to withdraw daily fatigue parties at CAPE HELLES. Transport due to leave tonight consists of the 4th to any special rendezvous. nothing to any special Division Report reports advance shelling of our front three guns put out of Range of left Coy horse was in enemy sniping. 2 men. Prevention of burst of enemy's into trenches of pavements & chewed &c. Transport land on 12/5/15 and 20th Supplies of B.Coy members Oxide. Capt Shout Coy returned to 2nd Rly Coy in trenches.	

10th May

WAR DIARY or INTELLIGENCE SUMMARY.

(Erase heading not required.)

Army Form C. 2118.

Hour, Date, Place	Summary of Events and Information	Remarks and references to Appendices
17th May 1915	Officer 26 other ranks left as for Marne Farm. Enemy heavy shell fire of infantry and assault attempted at 11-30 am. No damage at Battn H.Q. to a German shell. Two Battn officers arrived for 2 Bn Royal Irish were all wounded, containing 5 p.m.	
10 A.	Received 32 Bomb throwers and 32 bills for carrying stretchers, from Brigade H.Qrs. with a request that great care be taken of them. Received from Battalion orders:— Commendation:— "The following Warrant Officers, N.C.O.'s have been this forwarded commended by G.O.C. in C. New Enemy 6th Division for able & quick work during the heavy January to April 1915:— No. 28358 Col Major Woods A. " " Col S.Major Winder V.G. " 2965 Sergt Morley A. " 5203 Cpl Ryrant T.	

Army Form C. 2118.

WAR DIARY
or
INTELLIGENCE SUMMARY.
(Erase heading not required.)

Instructions regarding War Diaries and Intelligence Summaries are contained in F.S. Regs., Part II. and the Staff Manual respectively. Title pages will be prepared in manuscript.

Hour, Date, Place	Summary of Events and Information	Remarks and references to Appendices

1915

May 19th. Battalion begin to get allotted to be by General Jardin Staff of 9th Division. Huts are we settled. I am very I am but thanks by Colonel Cape Roberts been in trenches

May 30th 1/2 Coys of 11th Service Battalion Royal Scots accompanied Canadian battalion show trenches. Officers & all ranks put of I.O.I. involved. J. Watson Reports Residue Battalions attended from Red ... own trench strength. "not fighting"

No.15490. Pte. Harrison J. Bernhead by F.G.C.M. at K.O.J. Magazine charge "Asleep on his post"

No. 15490 Pte K.O.J. Pte. 16th Battalion attached for Instruction in trenches

II Coy. relieved A Coy in trenches

Forms/C. 2118/10

WAR DIARY
or
INTELLIGENCE SUMMARY.

(Erase heading not required.)

Army Form C. 2118.

Hour, Date, Place	Summary of Events and Information	Remarks and references to Appendices
1915 23rd May	[illegible] signed & declared war on ITALY No 2423 Pte. Steel A. [illegible] dangerously wounded in trench 3.20 p.m. Died on way to Divis. in Reserve Trenches. Fine day.	
24th May	ITALY declared war on AUSTRIA 6 Austrians, members of Engineers of 9 M. Bn. Slovakish Regt. found in dug-out & were sent into to Major [illegible] to Headqrs. in view of Italian attack. Nothing of importance happening. Weather continues very hot & calm. See below.	
25th May	14-3-15. No 1760 Ple. Sergt. J. Chay. 6 wound. left cheek. 1697 " Hoopper (B—) as wound Buttock sight. A. Coy. inward B. Coy. in trenches	

Army Form C. 2118.

WAR DIARY
or
INTELLIGENCE SUMMARY.
(Erase heading not required.)

Instructions regarding War Diaries and Intelligence Summaries are contained in F. S. Regs., Part II. and the Staff Manual respectively. Title pages will be prepared in manuscript.

Hour, Date, Place	Summary of Events and Information	Remarks and references to Appendices
1916 May 26.	Received orders to proceed to join 5th Infantry Brigade. Battalion had previously been reported by our aeroplanes to have moved by our own aeroplanes but intelligence only was obtained. (A) Battalion	
May 29th.	Hostile aeroplane sighted this afternoon, dropped a bomb in our G.S. gas, which set fire to some rations.	
26th May	Troops previous to date on march	

WAR DIARY
or
INTELLIGENCE SUMMARY.
(Erase heading not required.)

Army Form C. 2118.

Instructions regarding War Diaries and Intelligence Summaries are contained in F. S. Regs., Part II. and the Staff Manual respectively. Title pages will be prepared in manuscript.

Hour, Date, Place	Summary of Events and Information	Remarks and references to Appendices
1915 May 29th	An officer & 20 N.C.O.'s & 2/ Hoyal Regt. reinforcements. Inspection by C.O. in the time. Maj Gen. O'N. Congreve V.C. C.B., M.O., took over command of 6th Division.	
May 30th	2/ Gloucester Regt. in 60 men of Army Cyclist & Co. Regt. arrived, took over trench line about 10 p.m. Upon being relieved our Battalion assembled in field at cross roads & ran new road, 300 yrs east of Bn. H.Q. & F station dept ARMENTIERES 11-45 pm for BAILLEUL	

Army Form C. 2118.

WAR DIARY
or
INTELLIGENCE SUMMARY.
(Erase heading not required.)

Instructions regarding War Diaries and Intelligence Summaries are contained in F. S. Regs., Part II. and the Staff Manual respectively. Title pages will be prepared in manuscript.

Hour, Date, Place	Summary of Events and Information	Remarks and references to Appendices
1915 31st May	Battalion arrived at BAILLEUL at 8.30 a.m during the march. 31.30 Officers 945 other ranks. Accommodation in Billets. W. August arrived 18 signallers at 1-30 on 6th arriver from L. BAILLEUM. Lectures given demos to Officers and N.C.O's. Recognising Operation Order No. 1 from Brigade. W.R.Ogden. amn. capm. Sept 16 adjt. 1/5 L. N. Lancs Regt.	

151st Inf.Bde.
50th Div.

Battn. transferred
from 16th Inf.Bde.
6th Div. 11.6.15.

1/5th BATTN. THE LOYAL NORTH LANCASHIRE REGIMENT.

J U N E

1 9 1 5

Army Form C. 2118.

WAR DIARY
or
INTELLIGENCE SUMMARY.
(Erase heading not required.)

Instructions regarding War Diaries and Intelligence Summaries are contained in F.S. Regs, Part II. and the Staff Manual respectively. Title pages will be prepared in manuscript.

Hour, Date, Place	Summary of Events and Information	Remarks and references to Appendices
1st June 1915	Brigade reformed march & orders to be used on the march. Copy Commands & pass-words in Supl. 2 & 8 at 5.15 a.m. Batt. left Battalion with the Brigade and marched to ground about 1½ miles NW of POPERINGHE arriving about 10.30 a.m. Brigade marched in following order as per Operation Order No. 17. Advanced Guard: ½ of 11/K.S. B's, 16 & 4 Secs, and 1st London 4 Coy R.E. Main Body -- (a) Leicester Guns & Amm, Major Buchanan Dunlot Troops - one Coy. 1/Leicester Regt. (b) Main Body: Brigade Headquarters. 1/Leicester Regt - less 1 Coy - 2/York & Lancs, 1/K.S.L.I, 5/K.O.M.Lancs, 1/Buffs, 1/London Field Co R.E., 16 Fd Field Ambce. Bivouacked the night on ground allotted.	
June 2, 1915	Battalion rested on bivouac ground. All very pistols -11 in number-handed in to Brigade. Army Commander Gen Plumer visited our bivouac ground about 3.30 p.m. All packs were tidily arranged. Received 1500 rounds of .303 to draw from Brigade. At 6.30 p.m. Battn. commenced march of 12 miles to VLAMERTINGHE (H.S.R.) about 1½ miles NW of YPRES, proceeding via POPERINGHE and VLAMERTINGHE and arrived about 11.15 p.m. Transport proceeded to G.5.b. where all Brigade transport camped.	
June 3 1915	'C' Coy furnished 2 working parties each of 1 officer and 50 men for work with Leicesters and 1/York and Lancs respectively. One man wounded. 15944 Pte Tragg (C.S.W. Right Stowden). Very 7-battn attack not reported. Usual to Coys. 1 Machine gun Officer, Capt Gooson, with two m guns with detachments attached to York and Lancs Bn. in Wieltje (2½ miles NE of YPRES). Batn. made up to 1070 rounds of ammunition per man. Three officers fell in at our billets.	
June 4, 1915	Battn. moved into trenches NE of ST JEAN, relieving Somerset Light Infantry. Left half of Battalion at 9.30 p.m. Cd took over trenches 'C' 'D' Coys in advanced trenches 'A' Coy in second line. ('B' Coy and MGs) in third line at ST JEAN.	
June 5 1915	15162 Pte Powell killed (DCM): 2572 Pte Monks N Coy wounded. Enemy shelling immediate front.	

(9 29 6) W 4141-463 100,000 9/14 HWV Forms/C. 2118/10

Army Form C. 2118.

WAR DIARY
or
INTELLIGENCE SUMMARY.
(Erase heading not required.)

Instructions regarding War Diaries and Intelligence Summaries are contained in F. S. Regs., Part II. and the Staff Manual respectively. Title pages will be prepared in manuscript.

Hour, Date, Place	Summary of Events and Information	Remarks and references to Appendices
June 6. 1915.	Still in trenches. Pnte Nixon. G.S.W. head. Died 6 p.m. 2584. McEnnett "B" Cay killed. Sgt. Hill. 401 Sgt Roscoe W.G. "B" Cay wounded shall. hand and toe. 2 Sgts; 3975 Pte G. Hall 9.8. "B" Cay shall wound stomach; 1093 Sgt Pundy J.S. Cay shell wound knee; 1410 Pte Berner shell wound arm; 2401 Hope W.S. "D" Cay shell wound left eye under jaw; 3029 Packett W., "D" Coy. G.S.W. side. Heavy shelling of third line; also sniping. Received information that HQ of battalion was to be transferred to 151st Inf. Bde. 6 officers intimation as to boundaries 66.3/appd Panorama f 1 "D" Cay; killed G.S. 3313 Pte Hardy W. 1935 G.S.W. chest. dangerous. 2071 Pte Spargo J 1 "D" Cay. G.S.W. shoulder. Received information from Brigade 1/6/Capt J F Cauchin under orders for E. Kent Bn. to come in suite 8.30 p.m. at 19 k field amb. turned out to be N g maneuvered between WILTJE and...	
June 7. 1915	320 Pte Edwin J. G.S.W. arm slight. Sniper killed by light shell. commenced at 6.15 p.m. followed by 6 very heavy shells at 6 miles interval commenced at 6 p.m. H.E. and Shrapnel. heavy shelling between 7.30 and 8.30 p.m. all within an area of 160 yds. Intermittent shelling throughout night. One officer and 2 men attacked inoculation at BRANDHOEK in effectiveness of Respirators. Relieved in trenches by N. Stafford Regt. Moved out to that road to make 1/2 miles N.F. VLAMERTINGHE commencing at 10 p.m. First Company to be relieved arrived at 1.40 a.m. 10/6/15.	
June 8. 1915.		
June 9. 1915.		
June 10. 1915.	Moved off by Companies at 5 minute intervals and went 2 1/2 m. to camp en route. and for same time of the arrival at... GeorgianGen.IngouvilleWilliams gave of farewell address to Batt. During the 4/6th & 9/6th 1915. He did not attach officers and men of the 6th L.N. Lanc. Regt. I came here to say good bye. I am very sorry to lose the Batten from this Brigade which I just saw parted. I made up my mind that I have a good Battalion and well trained I made up my opinion was well... I can safely say that good work has been... thoroughly satisfactory 9 stch have fair pleasure in telling...	

Army Form C. 2118.

WAR DIARY
or
INTELLIGENCE SUMMARY.
(Erase heading not required.)

Instructions regarding War Diaries and Intelligence Summaries are contained in F.S. Regs., Part II. and the Staff Manual respectively. Title pages will be prepared in manuscript.

Hour, Date, Place	Summary of Events and Information	Remarks and references to Appendices
June 10 (cont) 1915	[illegible] Brigade [illegible] of [illegible] that you are going away, I am confident that as long as life & H. Lancs. Regt. Does [illegible], they will always keep their name, and do their utmost loyally and honestly. I wish you every success on your new sphere and shall be glad to bring your [illegible] with great interest. Received notification from 16th D.L.C. that No. 225 f. Sgt. Morley awarded D.C.M. Battn marched out of trenches bivouac and moved to G.17d (Map 28) 2 miles S.W. of VLAMERTINGHE. Battn in Brigade. High in form [illegible] to 151st (H) Bde. Brigadier Gen. inspected battalion in billets dress bivouac.	
June 11. 1915	Still at G.17d.	
June 12. 1915	Still at G.17d. Four M guns of Bn. under Capt Gurdon proceeded to	
June 13. 1915	front line of trenches at Hooge, where they relieved 4 M guns of Hooge CHATEAU garrison occupying trench.	
June 14. 1915	Still at G.17d. Bn. completed with smoke helmets.	
June 15. 1915	Still at G.17d. At 10.15 pm Battn moved from bivouac at G.17d. and proceeded to dug outs at BEKE H.23c. (Transport remained at bivouac G.17d.) Battn was in general reserve for attack on German trenches by 3rd Division.	
June 16. 1915	Battalion in reserve at HOOGE. Heavy bombardment by our Artillery of enemy position commencing at 2.50 pm. Two of our Machine Guns of Hooge did first rate work getting 3rd Division troops the first 3 lines of trenches, our M.gun staff finally but afterwards were compelled to withdraw to [illegible] [illegible] 1st Lieut. (157) [illegible] taken. [illegible] Bluer 2552, P2E 13m by E.J. [illegible] G.S.W. Lft, 2519 Pte Poulson R.H. Shrapnel head (C.Coy.) 2103 Pte Buncer, J.M. e'Coy, Unbearable. 149, Pte Parker shrapnel head	
June 17. 1915	Bn. received orders to reinforce Border Regt 1449. K. Brigade at 10 am and moved out of bivouac about 1.30 am. to Sanctuary Wood, 5 of Hooge and E. of ZILLE BEKE. B & D Coys in maple copse: 560 men of Battalion out supporting throughout the night. The [illegible] reported two Battn 2nd Bn. City of London Regt. casualties. 2763 Richard R. A.Coy. rtd. 2923 Pte Vickers, F.H. "A"Coy. Shell. scalp. 1639 Cpl. Weaver, C. "B"Coy. G.S.W. head. 1456 Sgt. Klemm, P. "e"Coy. G.S.W. hand. 560 Sgt. [illegible] P. "C"Coy. G.S.W. leg. 1370 Pte Harding J. "D"Coy. G.S.W. arm. 2325 Pte. Heavey, J. "A" Shell, face, slight.	

WAR DIARY or INTELLIGENCE SUMMARY

Army Form C. 2118.

Hour, Date, Place	Summary of Events and Information	Remarks and references to Appendices
June 18. 1915	Bn. disposed as for 17th. 3 Coys out as digging and carrying parties under R.E. on communication trench to HOOGE and also to ZOUAVE WOOD. Heavy bombardment of left of our position in Sanctuary Wood commencing at 7.30 p.m.	
June 19. 1915	Ptes Ball and Thomas buried in Sanctuary Wood. Ptes Cope 'B' 'D' Coys relieved S.K.N.T. in trenches 151 · 152 in Sanctuary Wood. Bn. came under orders of G.O.C. 9th Bde as soon as relief of 149th Bde was carried out. Capt Greenway R.O. and Machine Gun retired at Battn Headquarters. Casualties 2462 Pte Faulkner (Re). G.S.W. L side of duty. 1543 Pte Carson W. 'A' Coy G.S.W. R Shoulder. Bn relieved in Sanctuary Wood by Royal Fusiliers. 7149 Pte 3/2 Bn. Cave wounded on route. Casualties. 2622 Pte Worthington W. 'O' Coy Rifts? killed. 3218 Pte Casey G. 'B' Coy Rifts gsh ade ent. 2904 Pte Withrow F. 'A' Coy G.S.W. Rifts Knee. 3341 Pte Cave V. 'D' Coy G.S.W. Shoulder 673 Pte Dawes R. 'D' Coy. G.S.W. Shoulder.	
June 21. 1915	Moved from Bivouac to Bivouac field across road, vacated by H.L.I.	
June 22. 1915	Bn. moved at 8.30 a.m. and bivouacked in field about ½ mile S.E. of LOCRE and at dusk moved into huts between bivouac and LOCRE vacated by 4th Bn Seaforth Regt Bn inspected by Corps Commander Lieut. Gen. W. Ferguson in bivouac at 5.30 p.m. 1632 Pte Hill A. 'C' Co accidentally wounded by bullet from incinerator.	
June 23. 1915	Coys guarded 4 machine guns and rifles of Bn. for detachment moved to front line trenches at 5 p.m. Battn moved to bivouac at M36.b. at 7.30 p.m. (near DRANOUTRE)	
June 24–26. 1915	2nd at DRANOUTRE	
June 26. 1915	Moved at 11 a.m. to Bivouac camp – A & B Coys N.9.6.10's and C & D Coys N.20.c.3.5. The 5th Bn E. York Regt. took over bivouac which we vacated.	
June 27. 1915	Lieut Dickson relieved as water guard at Monne MOIR (M.25.b.) and conducted parties to new incineration under Transport lines. Battn. took up line of trenches 1½ miles W. of KEMPEL relieving 9th D.L.I. and 1st D. of 9th Durham L.I. Disposition as under. A Coy. C Coy. D Coy.	

79 — G.4. trench front; G.1 trench; G.2 trench; Reserve at Hornado Farm
3298 — G.4th; F.5; G.3; Reserve at Hornado Farm
Nos H.5 trench; S.E. No.10 ; S.P. 11
Battn H.Q. in house: H.Q. at KEMMEL.

Army Form C. 2118.

WAR DIARY
or
INTELLIGENCE SUMMARY.
(Erase heading not required.)

Instructions regarding War Diaries and Intelligence Summaries are contained in F.S. Regs, Part II. and the Staff Manual respectively. Title pages will be prepared in manuscript.

Hour, Date, Place	Summary of Events and Information	Remarks and references to Appendices
June 28. 1915	Report forwarded to Brigade on Smoke Helmets. Two working parties from "D" Coy, each of 1 Officer and 50 men for work with R.E. 6 to 9 p.m. & 1 midnight to 3 a.m. Casualties :- 1583 Pte Kelly H. slightly killed. 2391, Pte Gaskell * "A" Coy, 12370 Hurst E. 3051 Pte Newbury W. 12, C.of G.S. wounded slight on duty. 174 Pte Howes R "B" Coy. 2365: Pte Faulkner J "A" Coy. wounded slight on duty. 174 Pte Howes R "B" Coy, 3rd report today. Page 1637. Pte Stimson J. "B" Coy. 3rd report R. to arm.	
June 29. 1915	"D" Coy furnished 2 parties two for work with R.E. each of 1 NCO and 40 men and one of 1 Officer, 1 NCO and 50 men each for work at S.P. 11. "A" Coy relieved of Yard Trench H.Q. & was placed on Reserve Guard. "B" Coy. (comdd. 2/Lt) 8gt. Sunday. "C" Coy. G.S.W. right hand Coy. (comdd.) T.N.C.O. and 10 men for work with R.E.	
June 30. 1915	"D" Coy, furnished two working parties One of 1 Officer and 50 men for work with R.E. & two of 2 N.C.O. and 30 men for work on dugouts and communication trench. The name of 7/Pt Whitehead was submitted to Brigade for a course of instruction in adjutants duties. Commdts received through Brigade from Reversion authorising leave to Officers and other ranks. Lord Cavan, the new Divisional Commander, visited the trenches.	

G. Hesk H.f. Col.
Commdg 1/5 Royal N. Lancs Regt

151st Inf.Bde.
50th Div.

1/5th BATTN. THE LOYAL NORTH LANCASHIRE REGIMENT.

J U L Y

1 9 1 5

Army Form C. 2118.

WAR DIARY
or
INTELLIGENCE SUMMARY.
(Erase heading not required.)

Instructions regarding War Diaries and Intelligence Summaries are contained in F.S. Regs., Part II. and the Staff Manual respectively. Title pages will be prepared in manuscript.

Hour, Date, Place	Summary of Events and Information	Remarks and references to Appendices
1st July 1915. Kemmel.	Battn. in trenches. Five working parties provided, each of 2 N.C.Os and 20 men, for work under R.E. on Communication trenches. Part of 'B' Coys. trenches breached in four places by shell fire; during two hours shelling from 1 to 3. Casualties:- 3294, Pte Campbell W. 'C' Coy. G.S.W. head ; 4441 Baden J. 'C' Coy. G.S.W. hand - at duty; 2082 Pte Vincent. 'C' Coy. G.S.W. hand - at duty; 1902 Pte Gregory H. 'B' Coy. Shell side: 230 Pte Morgan J. 'B' Coy. G.S.W. R. knee. 2538 Sgt. Gordon C. 'B' Coy. Skin. e. forfingr- at duty; 1332 Sgt Brook J.E. 'C' Coy. bullet splinter. head - at duty.	
2nd July 1915 Kemmel	Battn. in trenches. two working parties of 2 N.C.Os and 20 men and 3 working parties of 1 N.C.O. and 10 men provided for work under R.E. on communication trenches.	
3rd July 1915 Kemmel	Battn. in trenches. Provided working parties of 3 N.C.Os and 60 men under R.E. The Battn. was relieved in the trenches by the 9TH. Durham. L.I.	
4th July 1915. LOCRE.	First party, consisting of 4 officers and 4 N.C.Os proceeded on leave. Officers:- Major A.H.C. Whalan, N.C.O.s:- Q.M.S. Weatly 'A' Co. Capt. Bt Major, W.R.H. Dann, Sgt. Ockensley 'D' Capt. C.K. Potter, Morley 'C' Capt. P.E. Pilling. Cpl. Maguire 'D'	
5th July 1915 LOCRE.	Battn. in Rutments.	
6th July 1915 LOCRE.	Capt. J. Entwisle attached to 2nd Buffs, for Adjutant's course.	
7th July 1915 LOCRE		
8th July 1915 LOCRE		
9th July 1915 LOCRE	At 9pm. Battn. relieved 9th Durham L.I. in trenches at KEMMEL. Battn. in trenches. The Corps Commander had a conference with the C Os of this Brigade. Working parties including 180 men were provided for digging. Casualties:- 2033, Pte. Hayward J. 'B' Coy. G.S.W. & forearm. slight duty. 1751, Pte J. Aylesbury " " Bayonet-arm - to duty. 2555 - Fray " Hutton cv. 6 'B' " G.S.W arm - to duty. 1298 - " " 'B' " killed in action 2561 - Marshall " 'B' " killed in action 2521 - Bean J.E. " 'B' " Rifle grenade (prem. expl) body&arms. 2595 - Watmough N.P. 'B'. R. arm.	
10 July 1915 KEMMEL		

Army Form C. 2118.

WAR DIARY
or
INTELLIGENCE SUMMARY.
(Erase heading not required.)

Hour, Date, Place	Summary of Events and Information	Remarks and references to Appendices
11 July 1915 KEMMEL	Battn in trenches. 150 men provided for digging purposes under R.E. Casualties:- 2477 Pte Brophy M. "B" Coy. Rifle grenade chin. at duty. 1696 Pte Gibson J. "C" - G.S.W. Upper lip - at duty.	
12 July 1915 KEMMEL 13 July 1915 Near LOCRE →	Battn relieved from trenches by the 2nd & 6th Yorks, and moved back to bivouac near LOCRE. Move completed by 3 a.m. of the 13 inst. 3 working parties supplied for digging including 3 officers and 160 other ranks, also fatigue party of 3 officers and 158 other ranks supplied. Brigade Gen'l inspected complete turnout of horse transport at 4 p.m. S.P. 9-10 taken over from 7TH D.f.d. by two peletons of "D" Coy. Casualties 414. Pte Morris J. "B" Coy. H.E. Shell - hand Reg. died of w. 15/7/15 2659 - Wilkinson J. "B" - - - R.Leg 1899 - Turton J. "A" - - - R. arm - at duty 1858 - Hveden J. "B" - - -	
14 July 1915. Near LOCRE	Working parties for digging under R.E. supplied, including 5 officers & 360 other ranks	
15 July 1915. Near LOCRE	Received orders at 9 p.m. to be ready to move at 15 minutes notice. Machine guns relieved from trenches. Also S.P. 9-10 relieved. Casualties:- 2390 Pte Cowan P.N. "C" Co. G.S.W. L hand, accidental - duty. 1268 - Small J. J. "D" - - - L foot. accidental.	
16 July 1915. Near LOCRE.	Brigade moved from LOCRE to PONT DE NIEPPE commencing at 8.15 p.m and marching in the order:- Bde Hd qtp 8.15 p.m 9 10 R 9 8.17 p.m 6/8 10 R 9 8.21 p.m 7 10 R 9 8.25 p.m 5 Loyal N Lanc. 8.29 p.m 1st line Transport 8.33 p.m. under command of Major Sneddle.	

Army Form C. 2118.

WAR DIARY or INTELLIGENCE SUMMARY.

(Erase heading not required.)

Instructions regarding War Diaries and Intelligence Summaries are contained in F.S. Regs., Part II. and the Staff Manual respectively. Title pages will be prepared in manuscript.

Hour, Date, Place		Summary of Events and Information	Remarks and references to Appendices
17 July 1915	PONT DE NIEPPE	Battn. billeted in cheffre. commencing at 6.30 p.m. battn. moved into ARMENTIERES occupying HOSPICE CIVIL, RUE DE PATURES, Battn. HdQrs 35 RUE DE NATIONALE. 'C' Coy. attached to 6/8 Durham L.I. and occupied reserve trenches on left of LILLE RD. 3 machine guns occupied M trenches, 2 guns in No 72 trench, 1 gun in No 71 trench. Cpl. Snelham attended a M.G. course.	
18 July 1915	ARMENTIERES	Forwarded air reconnaissance report to the Brigade. The Brigadier, Col. F.S.M. Shea. C.B., D.S.O., inspected billets of Battalion at 4.30 p.m. Carrying party of 1 officer and 60 other ranks furnished for carrying mining stores to trench 67.	
19 July 1915	ARMENTIERES	Orders received to have one company always ready, until further orders, to turn out at 15 minutes notice.	
20 July 1915	ARMENTIERES	Cpl. Taylor 'C' Coy. proceeded to Base at HAVRE for duty. 36 Grenadiers reported at the Battn. Headquarters, to Brigade Grenadier Officer for instruction and training.	
21 July 1915	ARMENTIERES	Major Haslam acted as President, and Capt. Smith as member of a F.G.C.M. assembled at Battn. HdQtrs. at 10 a.m. 'C' Company relieved in reserve trenches by 7th Warwicks. The C.O. and Adjutant visited trenches to be taken over by Battn. on the night of 24/25 inst. Fatigue party of 24 officers and 200 other ranks detailed for work on communication trench.	
22 July 1915	ARMENTIERES	'A' Coy. 2 officers 100 other ranks. 'B' Coy. 2 officers 100 other ranks. Captain K. Potter acted as member of F.G.C.M. assembled at HdQrs 7th Durham L.I. at 10 a.m. Casualties 2492 Pte. Barrow J. (M. gunner) 'C' Coy. G.S.W. R. wrist & R. thigh.	
23 July 1915	ARMENTIERES	Battn. still in HOSPICE CIVIL.	
24 July 1915	ARMENTIERES	Battn. relieved 6/8 Durham L.I. in trenches to left of LILLE ROAD, facing WEZ MACQUART. 'A' Coy. occupying 67 trench, 'B' - 68 - 'C' - 69 - 'D' - 70 - Two Coys 6/8 Durham L.I. in support 1 company occupying LILLE POST and the other occupying SUPPORTING LINE.	

Army Form C. 2118.

WAR DIARY
or
INTELLIGENCE SUMMARY.
(Erase heading not required.)

Instructions regarding War Diaries and Intelligence Summaries are contained in F.S. Regs., Part II. and the Staff Manual respectively. Title pages will be prepared in manuscript.

Hour, Date, Place		Summary of Events and Information	Remarks and references to Appendices
25 July 1915	ARMENTIERES.	Brigade instructed that all officers should make themselves acquainted with the streets of ARMENTIERES. Casualties:- 2273 Pte Smith F. "D" Coy. Killed in action. 1874 — Blackburn S. "B". — G.S.W. leg, slight, at duty.	
26 July 1915	ARMENTIERES	Battn in trenches. Plan of ARMENTIERES issued to each Coy. Received report re wastage in ammunition, and instructions to practise more economy in the matter of ammunition.	
27 July 1915	ARMENTIERES	Brigadier visited the trenches and expressed his approval of them. 3 officers of 9th 10 R.J. attached to Battn. for 19 days instructions. Lt Miller 6/8 D.L.I attached (M Gun officer) Killed in action.	
28 July 1915	ARMENTIERES	Battn. in trenches. Casualties:- 2924 Pte Grealy E. "B" Coy. Died of wounds. LILLE POST and SUPPORTING LINE. The G. Co. C. (Lord Cavan) Division, inspected 10 a.m. 2 Coys. 6/7 10 R.J. General Clifford visited trenches by 2 Coys. 9TH 10 R.J. Lt. Cox, R.E. attached off support, relieved Casualties :- 2420 Pte Richardson C. "D" Coy. Killed in action. 2341 — Anderson H. "A". — G.S.W. head — DUTY. 1311 Lt Muason & Co. "A". — Rifle Grenade — left arm. 2164 Cpl Curwekaid G. "A". — G.S.W. — left arm. 2164 Pte Gilpin W. "A". — Killed in action. 2792 — Kirkman J. "A". — Rifle grenade — Ram body	
29 July 1915	ARMENTIERES	Battn. in trenches. Our transport moved from RUE DE COLLEGE to field in 24 D 3.7. Casualty 2555 Pte Fray J. "B" Coy. Died of wounds	
30 July 1915	ARMENTIERES	Battn. in trenches.	
31 July 1915	ARMENTIERES.	Battn. in trenches. The Corps Commander Sir Charles Ferguson, visited our line. Slight bombardment of german trenches in front of town, during afternoon and evening germans replied rather feebly. Casualty:- Lt Chapman A.R.B. "D" Coy. Severe motor b'face.	

WRD Adam Lt. Col. Cmdg. 1/5 Loyal N Lancashire Regt.

151st Inf.Bde.
50th Div.

1/5th BATTN. THE LOYAL NORTH LANCASHIRE REGIMENT.

A U G U S T

1 9 1 5

Army Form C. 2118.

WAR DIARY
or
INTELLIGENCE SUMMARY.
(Erase heading not required.)

1/5 Loyal Lancs Regt

Place	Date	Hour	Summary of Events and Information	Remarks and references to Appendices
ARMENTIERES	1 Aug. 1915		Battn relieved in trenches by 6th Bn. Northumberland Fusiliers in trench 69; 7th Bn. N.F. in trenches 68 + 69; and 5th Bn. Border Regt. in trench 70; each taking over support lines. Battn went into billets as follows: 'A' Coy. occupied small factory near ÉCOLE PROFESSIONNELLE; 'B' Coy. occupied 'RUE DE COLLEGE'. 'C' & 'D' Coys occupied the Convent.	
—	2 —		Battn in billets. 2/Lt. Richardson proceeded to BAILLEUL to undergo course on machine gun.	
—	3 —		The Brigadier visited billets.	
—	4 —		Provided 44 working parties in subsidiary line:- One officer and 50 men from 'D' Coy. at 8 a.m.; One: two officers and 100 men from 'C' Coy at 7.30 p.m. — 'D' — 8.30 a.m. — 'B' — 7.30 p.m.	
			'A' Coy. furnished 50 men for inlying picquet for duty if required, with Fire Brigade. Battalion in billets. Casualty. No. 2253 Pte Crompton R. 'B' Co Shrapnel R. eye — AT DUTY	
—	5 —		2/Lt. R.S. Entwisle and 2/Lt. Ernest Blackburn joined Battn. from base.	
—	6 —		2/Lt. Hargreaves and 2/Lt. Edward Blackburn joined Battn. from base. Battn. relieved 5th Yorks and part of 4th Yorks in trenches 75, 76, 77, and support line, also SP.Y's & SP.Z.: 'A' Coy. occupied support line, 'B' Coy occupied trench 76; 'C' Coy occupied	
—	7 —		trench 77.	
—	8 —		Sgt. Busby and 19 men of 'C' Coy. attached to No. 2 Coy. R.E., 50th Division, for duty. Lt. Long W, joined Battn from base.	
—	9 —		Capt. Gherson attended Enquiry held by Claims Commission on Claim for billets. Woods. Brigadier inspected trenches at 10 a.m. Casualty: - No. 2368, Pte Hargreaves J. 'A' Coy, G.S.W. R.forearm.	
—	10 —		Received 3 Steel helmets from Brigade for experimental purposes. trench 75 shelled one shell obtained direct shot at a barricade. 3 men Kit by splinters. Casualties :- No.1884, Pte Blackburn S. 'B' Coy. Shrapnel - back, arm, shoulder. — 2322 — Sheffield Jo. 'B' Coy. R. eye. — 2278 — Luther H. 'B' — L. ankle	
—	11 —		Notice received from Brigade that leave for N.C.O's and men could be extended to five days from the present four days. Trench 76 again shelled and repairs to barricade + hut previous ally Knock down.	
—	12 —		Pte Lofton and Fielding 'A' Coy, fired by F.G.C.M. assembled at the ASYLUM at 3.30 p.m. Brigadier visited trenches. Casualties :- No. 1875 Pte Starrock J. 'D' Coy. Shell - head. — 1465 — Popplewell W. 'D' — R. Buttock - slight - AT DUTY — 1656 — Davies — Shrapnel - slight — AT DUTY	

Army Form C. 2118.

1/5 Loyal Lancs [?]

WAR DIARY
or
INTELLIGENCE SUMMARY
(Erase heading not required.)

Place	Date	Hour	Summary of Events and Information	Remarks and references to Appendices
ARMENTIERES	13 Aug 1915		Battn. relieved by 4th Bn. Durham Light Infantry in trenches and took up billets in the ASYLUM. Battalion in Brigade Reserve.	
			Casualties:- No 11470 Pte Holdsworth J. 'B' Coy. KILLED IN ACTION	
			— 181 — Cawley L. 'B' — KILLED IN ACTION	
			— 2477 2/Cpl Brophy M. 'B' — Shell — head	
			— 1435 Pte Brooks J. 'B' — — face	
			— 121 — Barnes W. 'B' — — R. wrist	
	14 —		125 from each of 'A', 'B', and 'C' Coys went to Baths at PONT DE NIEPPE. Court Martial proceedings on the case of Lofts and Feeling promulgated.	
	15 —		'A' Coy furnished a working party of 2 N.C.Os and 50 men.	
	16 —		'B' and 'C' Coys provided parties of 58 men each for digging with R.E.	
	17 —		'D' Coy furnished two working parties of 1 N.C.O. and 28 men each for work with R.E. Lt. W.G. Giblin, R.A.M.C. attached to Battn. vice Lt. J.W. Atkins R.A.M.C. transferred.	
	18 —		'A' Coy. provided a working party of 1 officer and 75 men, and 'B' and 'C' Coys parties of 1 officer and 50 men each, for work with R.E.	
	19 —		Battn. moved from the dogium. 'A' and 'B' Coys. occupying the Convent, and 'C' 'D' Coys RUE DE COLLEGE. Capt. Grierson joined 151st Inf. Bde. Staff as Bde. Machine Gun Officer. No 1273 Pte H. Lane 'D' Coy. went to Brigade to undertake the handling of pigeons. Major A.H.C. Hadow officer of the day. Capt. C.R. Potter promoted Major.	
	20 —		Casualty:- No 2123, Pte A.G. Fearn, 'A' Coy. Shrapnel-head-slight. AT DUTY. Major C.R. Potter officer of the day. 'D' Coy. furnished party of 1 N.C.O. and 20 men for work with R.E.	
	21 —		Divisional swimming baths allotted to Battn. from 9 a.m. till 12 noon. 'D' Coy provided a party of 20 men for work with R.E. 2/Lts. Cromwell H. Hargreaves & B. Blackburn Edward, and Blackburn Ernest, attended a 4 days class with the 1st Field Coy. R.E.	
	22		Battalion in billets.	
	23		Lecture to platoon officers at the Bde workshop on "French Warfare" by Capt. E.R. Clayton, Bde-Major.	

Army Form C. 2118.

WAR DIARY
or
INTELLIGENCE SUMMARY.
(Erase heading not required.)

1/5 Loyal N Lanc Regt

Instructions regarding War Diaries and Intelligence Summaries are contained in F.S. Regs., Part II. and the Staff Manual respectively. Title pages will be prepared in manuscript.

Place	Date	Hour	Summary of Events and Information	Remarks and references to Appendices
ARMENTIERES	24 August 1915	—	Brigadier inspected Billets of Battalion at 4.30 p.m.	
	25	—	Battn took over trenches 68, 69, and 70, and Support trenches on left of LILLE ROAD. 'A' Coy. in trench 68; 'C' Coy. in trench 69; 'D' Coy in trench 70; 'B' Coy in supporting line. Relief completed by 10.20 p.m.	
	26	—	Battn in trenches. Bde. replied for name of N.C.O. to fill vacancy of Q.M. Sgt. at Base. No 415, Sgt. J. Ball recommended. Casualty:- No 2737, Pte Graham J; 'A' Coy; G.S.W. head - slight - AT DUTY.	
	27	—	Battn in trenches. Wind - East. Special precautions taken against possible use of gas by the enemy.	
	28	—	Battn in trenches. G.O.C. Division visited the trenches. Casualties:- No 1560 Pte H.G. Williams, 'D' Coy. G.S.W. head - DIED OF WOUNDS
— 2174 Cpl M. Cavuck 'B' — KILLED IN ACTION.
— 1413 Pte W.B. Partington 'A' — G.S.W. L arm
— 2883 — J. Haythornwaite 'A' — G.S.W. R thigh	
	29	—	Battn in trenches. Brigadier visited the trenches. Slight bombardment of enemy's lines by our Artillery. No 27.22 Pte J. Hulme reported for Duty to 2nd Army	
	30	—	Battn in trenches. Worked at as per Bde Orders (SL.52J)	
	31	—	Battn in trenches. 'D' Coy relieved by 6th Durham L.I. and billeted at the ASYLUM. At last moment 'D' Coy ordered to remain in trenches till following morning in case of an attack. Casualties:- No 2380 Pte J. Weymes, 'A' Coy. G.S.W. L hand
— 1452 — J. Preston, 'D' — KILLED IN ACTION.	

W. Watson Lt Major
O.C. 1/5 Loyal N Lanc Regt

151st Inf.Bde.
50th Div.

1/5th BATTN. THE ROYAL NORTH LANCASHIRE REGIMENT.

S E P T E M B E R

1 9 1 5

WAR DIARY or INTELLIGENCE SUMMARY.

Army Form C. 2118

1/5 LOYAL N. LANCASHIRE RGT

(Erase heading not required.)

Place	Date	Hour	Summary of Events and Information	Remarks and references to Appendices
ARMENTIERES	Sept.1.1916		'B' Coy. supplied two working parties, one of 1 officer and 80 men (carrying) and one of 1 officer and 140 men, with 35 shovels and 5 picks, for work with R.E. at 7.30p.m. 'A' Coy. furnished 1 officer and 50 men for carrying with R.E. at LEITH WALK, 9p.m. Received reinforcement of one man from Rouen. 2.Lut J.W. Long, Sgt. J. Ball, and Sgt. J. Grist recommended for appointments as instructors at 2nd Army School of Instruction.	
	-2			
	-3		'A' Coy. furnished carrying party of 1 officer and 30 men for work with R.E. at PORTE EGAL dump at 8.30 a.m. 'A' Coy. held furnished the following parties for R.E. 1 officer and 50 men at 7.30p.m.; 30 men with 15 shovels and 5 picks at 7.30p.m.; 1 officer and 50 men for carrying at LEITH WALK, 9p.m.	
	-4		'D' Coy. supplied following working parties for R.E. 1 officer and 60 men with 58 shovels and 10 picks at 7.30p.m. 1 - 35 - - - 7.30pm 1 - 15 - - - 7.30pm 1 - 20 - for carrying purposes at 7.30pm 'A' Coy. supplied following working parties for R.E. 1 officer and 25 men for carrying at LEITH WALK, 9p.m. - 40 - - HAYSTACK FARM, 9p.m. Lieut. H.A. Rieckerdsen recommended for appointment as Adjutant, School of Instruction. 'A' Coy took over billet at CORDON warehouse, RUE DE COLBERT. 'B' Coy took over billet at LOURME warehouse, BOULEVARDE FARDNERBE 'C' - - - - VILLARD - - STRASBOURG, - DUFOUR DAREN 'D' - - - - RUE DE LA GARE, warehouse, RUE DE LA GARE.	
	5. 6.			
	7		Regtl. Grenadiers, Signallers, Police, & Pioneers were billeted with 'D' Coy. The G.O.C. 2nd Army, inspected the Battalion on ground in RUE SADI CARNOT at 11.45 a.m.	
	8		1 Officer and 50 men were provided by each Coy. for harvesting. 'B' and 'C' Coys. also furnished parties of 1 officer and 50 men each for carrying with R.E. at 9 p.m.	

Army Form C. 2118

WAR DIARY
or
INTELLIGENCE SUMMARY
(Erase heading not required.)

1/5 LOYAL N. LANCASHIRE REGT

Place	Date	Hour	Summary of Events and Information	Remarks and references to Appendices
ARMENTIERES	Sept 9/1915		2/Lts R.R. Hackatt, E.A. Ward, C. Marshall, and R.D.B. Sparkes were detailed to attend a course in military engineering, and reported to Capt. Stowell at the ASYLUM at 10 a.m. Lecture given to Officers on minor tactics of trench warfare.	
	-10		Swimming trophies were allotted as under:- "B" Coy. 1 p.m to 2 p.m. "D" Coy. 2 p.m to 3 p.m. "C" Coy. 3 p.m to 4 p.m. "A" Coy. 4 p.m to 5 p.m. Coys provided 1 officer and 50 men each for harvesting. Lecture as on previous day. Major Potter detailed as President of a F.G.C.M. held at Hd.Qtrs of 6th D.L.I. at 4 p.m. Coys provided 1 officer and 50 men each for harvesting.	
	-11		Lecture as on previous day. Coys provided 1 officer and 50 men each for harvesting. Also each Coy provided 1 officer and 50 men for trench work with 142nd Coy R.E.	
	-12		Two Machine guns took up position in Subsidiary Line. Battn. moved to billets in HOSPICE CIVIL, RUE DE ROTOURS.	
	-13		"A" and "D" Coys provided 1 officer and 50 men each for carrying with R.E. at 8 p.m.	
	-14		"B" and "C" Coys provided 1 officer and 50 men each for carrying with R.E. at 8 p.m.	
	-15		"A" Coy. furnished party of 1 officer and 50 men for work with R.E. at 8 p.m. "B" Coy. provided a cellaying party of 1 Officer and 50 men for work with R.E. at LEITH WALK, 8 p.m.	
	-16		Capt. J. Entwisle detailed as member of a F.G.C.M. held at 142 RUE NATIONALE, 3 p.m. Lts. N. Dickinson and W.C. Walley returned from duty with R.E. "C" Coy. provided carrying party of 1 officer and 50 men for work with R.E. at LEITH WALK, 8 p.m. 2 p.m. to 3 p.m. Baths at PONT NIEPPE allotted to Battalion 11.15 a.m. to 12 noon, 2 p.m. to 3 p.m. and 4 p.m. to 5 p.m.	

Army Form C. 2118

WAR DIARY
or
INTELLIGENCE SUMMARY.
(Erase heading not required.)

1/5 LOYAL N. LANCASHIRE REGT

Place	Date	Hour	Summary of Events and Information	Remarks and references to Appendices
ARMENTIERES	Sept 17 1915		'A' Coy provided carrying party of 1 Officer and 50 men for work with R.E. at LEITH WALK, 8 p.m.	
	- 18		Swimming Baths allotted to Battn from 8am to 12 noon, and from 2 to 4 p.m. The C.O. visited the General at Bde. HdQrs 3 p.m. Sgt Busby and L/Cpl Markland instructed to interview the Brigadier-General at 2 p.m. and 2.45 p.m. respectively. Battalion took over trenches. 75 ('B' Coy) 76 ('A' Coy) 77 ('D' Coy) Support ('C' Coy). Relief completed 9.45 p.m. Casualties: Pte Lever, T.W. 'A' Co. killed in action.	
	- 19		No 2007 g. In the trenches. Trench 75, and right of trench 76, shelled by whizz bangs and trench howitzers in the early morning. Casualties. No 1629 Pte Mallett R.S. 'A' Co. G.S.W. L forearm. — 130 Cpl Connor J. 'C' — Shrapnel L hand.	
	- 20		In the trenches. Line bombarded from 7am to 7.50 a.m. by whizz bangs, stink shells, shrapnel and larger shells. Very little damage done. Our artillery bombarded BLACK REDOUBT about 4 p.m. Casualties No 3010 Pte Edge T. 'B' Co. Shrapnel L side & back. Lieut Blackburn Ernest 'A' — L buttock.	
	- 21		In the trenches. Special report on 'Work for completion' in trenches 75, 76, and 77, forwarded to 157 Inf Bde. Casualties No 1745 Pte Rayner f. 'B' Co. Shrapnel, forefinger - AT DUTY.	
	- 22		In the trenches	

Army Form C. 2118

WAR DIARY
or
INTELLIGENCE SUMMARY.
(Erase heading not required.)

1/5 LOYAL N. LANCASHIRE REGT.

Instructions regarding War Diaries and Intelligence Summaries are contained in F.S. Regs., Part II. and the Staff Manual respectively. Title pages will be prepared in manuscript.

Place	Date	Hour	Summary of Events and Information	Remarks and references to Appendices
ARMENTIERES	Sept 23 1915		In the trenches. Battn relieved in trenches by 5th Border Regt, and proceeded to Billets in Armentieres 'H' area. Casualties Pte McCoy T. 'A' Co. Shrapnel, head.	
			No 2290 Pte McCoy T. 'A' Co. Shrapnel, head.	
			— 3207 — Hulme W. 'D' — face, body, limbs.	
			— 1266 — Roberts R. 'A' — R. wrist — AT DUTY	
			— 2611 — Evans J. 'A' — l. ear — AT DUTY	
	24		Instructions received for sandbags to be drawn at the rate of two per man. Notification received from Bde. that all men must be in billets by 8 p.m., and Battn must be ready to move at one hour's notice.	
	25		News received re progress near HOOGE and LA BASSÉE. Major A.H.C. Haslam detailed as President of F.G.C.M. held at Battn Hdqrs.	
	26		Battn moved into trenches at HOUPLINES. 'B' Coy and part of 'A' Coy, took over trench 88, 'C' Coy., trench 89., 'D' Coy S.S. 88. Hdqtrs of 8th R.F. taken over.	
HOUPLINES	27		In the trenches. Maj.-General P.S. Wilkinson, C.B., C.M.G., Cmdg 50th Division went round trenches. Leave suspended until further notice.	
			Casualties	
			No 976. Sgt Morris Q. 'C' Coy. killed in action.	
			— 1654. Pte. Edwards J. 'A' — G.S.W. abdomen	
			— 2262. A/Sgt Baron H. 'C' — Shell - l. side, chest	
			— 1648. Pte. Simpson W. 'C' — head	
	28		In the trenches. Sgt Laberer attended Divisional HdQtrs., for instruction in SACK's breathing apparatus.	

Army Form C. 2118.

WAR DIARY
or
INTELLIGENCE SUMMARY. 1/5 LOYAL N. LANCASHIRE REGT.

Place	Date	Hour	Summary of Events and Information	Remarks and references to Appendices
HOOPLINES	Sept 29, 1915		In the trenches. Sgt W. Tyldesley instructed to report at Div. HdQrs to give instruction in the use of bombs, to new troops.	
	-	30	Received copy of letter from Lord Kitchener, congratulating the troops on the recent advance.	

W R Dunn
Major.
fn OC 1/5 L. N. Lancs Regt.

151st Inf.Bde.
50th Div.

1/5th BATTN. THE LOYAL NORTH LANCASHIRE REGIMENT.

O C T O B E R

1 9 1 5

WAR DIARY or INTELLIGENCE SUMMARY

Army Form C. 2118.

(Erase heading not required.)

Place	Date	Hour	Summary of Events and Information	Remarks and references to Appendices
Trenches C.11.c.4.8.	1st Oct. 15		Still in trenches 88 & 89. 23rd Div. on our left, other side River L+S. 7th D.L.I on our right.	
	2nd Oct. 15		Trenches bombarded by enemy and rifle grenades during afternoon. Draft of 25 other ranks joined from No 4 entrenching Batt. Casualties: 1676 Pte. Gibson J. — C. Coy. Shrapnel wound, left upper leg. 1325 " Horton J. — A. " Shell, right arm, slight. 2100 " McDonald J. — A. " " right arm, slight. 2155 " " " — A. " " left arm, slight.	
	3rd Oct. 15		D. Coy. relieved B. Coy. in front line trench 88. 23.45 Pte. W. Sutton — C. Coy. Killed G.S.	
	4th Oct. 15		Cpl. Ware "A" Coy. instructed to report to 2nd Army Hd. Qrs. for course of instruction in Intelligence Police duty. Leave reopened.	
	5th Oct. 15		The Y.O.C. Division inspected trenches during morning.	
	7th Oct. 15		Extract from Intelligence Report:— "Patrol from trench 88 (D. Coy.) brought in German rifle and ammunition." 622 L/Cpl. J. Bayley — D. Coy. Killed G.S. 1049 L/C a. Partington — C. " " G.S.	
	8th Oct. 15		10 other ranks to reported at Divisional grenade school for instruction in bomb throwing.	

WAR DIARY or INTELLIGENCE SUMMARY

Army Form C. 2118.

(Erase heading not required.)

Place	Date	Hour	Summary of Events and Information	Remarks and references to Appendices
C.11.c.4.3. Trenches.	10. Oct. 1915		1/C.S.M. Fyldesleys C.Coy instructed to report at Divisional Grenade School for instruction in bomb throwing. One Coy of 1/2 D.LI. attached for instruction in trenches. Distribution:- One Platoon with each of our Coys. A Coy relieved B Coy in trenches, B Coy occupying SS 88.	
	11th Oct. 15		2/Lt Fox proceeded to 1st Army Grenade School. 1st R.D. = 6th K.M. for course of instruction in "Grenades".	
	12th Oct. 15		Relieved 1/S Worcester's 3 pl. between 7 am & 9 am. 4/C.S.M. Watkins C Coy attended office of D.D.S.T. Farm. Recd. 5 A Boy (?) G.S.W. neck and fracture. casualties:- 2967 Pte. Reeves " " of left eyelid.
30174 Poole-Style "   B. Boy G.S.W. head (Died 13/15)
3080 " Ainsley " C. " G.S.W. left shoulder.	
	13th Oct. 15		Enemys line bombarded facing trench 84 from 2 pm to 3.30 pm. after which smoke bombs were thrown by us along whole line. Smoke appeared to travel successfully and enemy opened heavy rifle and machine gun fire on our trenches, though their artillery retaliation appeared very weak. German lines appeared to be strongly held.	
			Casualties:- 1617 Hutchinson J. C Coy. G.S.W. thigh.
9099 Thomas J. " " G.S.W. head.
1714 Pte. Wall E. " " G.S.W. head + arm.
348 " Whittle W. " A " shell head & arm.
2360 " Smith W. " A " G.S.W. right hand.
2294 " Johnwood J. " A " Smoke bomb - burn.
6041 C/Sgt Bayliss J. " A " Killed G.S.	

A.D.S.S/Forms/C. 2118.

WAR DIARY
or
INTELLIGENCE SUMMARY.
(Erase heading not required.)

Army Form C. 2118.

Place	Date	Hour	Summary of Events and Information	Remarks and references to Appendices
Trenches 2/1 C.H.B	1915 15th Oct.		2 Platoons and one machine gun section of 13th Northumberland Fusiliers attached for instruction. Lt. Col. Garnett admitted to 1/1st Northumberland Field Ambulance suffering from Pyrexia. Major Dawn took over command of Battalion. Capt. Tathul showing during agonising. 2123 Pte Fearn "A" Coy. G.S.W. left side & left arm.	
	16th Oct.		No. 4/15 Sergt. I.T. Ball proceeded to N.C.O's School at ZUYTPEENE to take over duty as Instructor.	
	17th Oct.		Casualties :- 4410 Pte. Gaskin W. C Coy. G.S.W. right shoulder. 2216 Pte. Jackson J. B " Bayonet cut, right upper arm, accidental. 2062 " Maloney J. D " Killed - G.S.	
	18th Oct.		Corps Commander visited trenches. 2294 Pte Shickman W. C Coy. G.S.W. left upper arm.	
	19th Oct.		One Coy. of 13th Northumberland Fusiliers attached for 48 hours instruction. Lt. Col. Garnett proceeded to England.	
	20th Oct.		No. 6. 2/8th Division visited trenches having special attention to Coy. 13th N.F.	
	22nd Oct.		1965 Pte Waller J & 1836 Croney G " C" Coy. killed G.S. Relieved and proceeded to England to return to T.F.3 War office. Coy of 13th Northumberland Fusiliers relieved. 2511 Pte Oakes J. "C" Coy. killed G.S. 1890 " Brown J. "D" G.S.W. fingers, right hand.	
	23rd Oct.		Four cadets attached for 24 hours instruction in trench duty.	

WAR DIARY
INTELLIGENCE SUMMARY

Army Form C. 2118.

Place	Date	Hour	Summary of Events and Information	Remarks and references to Appendices
Trenches C.11.c.14.3	1915 24th Oct.		Capt. Whitehead took over Coy. duty as Adjt.	
	25th Oct.		Drew bomb carrying parties from Bn.	
	26th Oct.		2 Platoons of 1st Somerset Light Infy. attached for 48 hours instruction.	
	27th Oct.		Capt. Whitehead & Sergt. Gniot with 32 other ranks went by motor to Bailleul for the Kings Inspection. Returned by motor 6.30 p.m.	
			C.O. visited machine gun school at WISQUES.	
	28th Oct.		B.C. & D. Coys relieved in 88 and 89 trenches by R.B.R.J. A Coy remained in L.S. line. Battalion billeted in TISSAGE, HOUPLINES.	
	29th Oct.		In billets - resting.	
	30th Oct.		Major Potter returned off leave, took over duties of Adjutant. Battalion provided working parties under R.E. and Coys were allotted following coordinates:- B Coy 90 } to be supplied C " 90 } daily D " 90 }	
			No. 2331 L/C Lynes Lynes proceeded to WISQUES for course of instruction on machine Guns. Casualties:- 2038 Pte. Fea. A Coy. Shell – Wound. 2591 " Sherwood J. A Coy. Shell – Wound.	

P.O. Read Capt
a/adjt 7/5 L.N. Lanc Regt

151st Inf.Bde.
50th Div.

1/5th BATTN. THE LOYAL NORTH LANCASHIRE REGIMENT.

N O V E M B E R

1 9 1 5

WAR DIARY
or
INTELLIGENCE SUMMARY.

(Erase heading not required.)

Army Form C. 2118.

Place	Date	Hour	Summary of Events and Information	Remarks and references to Appendices
Houplines	1st Novr. 1915		All in billets at TISSAGE, HOUPLINES. 2/Lt. Hargreaves and 4 N.C.O.'s who do Scouts on Intelligence work attended lecture at 3 p.m. at Divisional Headquarters on "Observation work and German uniforms. Brigadier interviewed 2536 L/Sgt. C.S. Haynes 7 a.m.	
"	2nd Novr.	7 p.m.	Lieut. No. 2510 L/Cpl. Royley/ H. interviewed by the Brigadier General 7 p.m.	
Trenches C.11.c.4.3 to C.17.c.3.2. Sheet 36.	3rd Novr.		B, C, & D Coys. left billets at TISSAGE, HOUPLINES, and took over trenches 88 and 89 (B & D Coys. 88, and C Coy. 89) C.11.c.4.3. to C.17.c.3.2. On account of heavy rains trenches were in wretched condition. Close support trenches Hood and RIVER AVENUE (6.89 Trench) completely blocked by fallen earth. Footbridge over L/S under water and not usable by patrols.	
"	4th Novr.		2/Lt. Hargreaves interviewed by Major Battye at R.E. H.Q. D.L.I. at 2 p.m. re Intelligence work. 2/Lt. Hargreaves interviewed. Casualties:- 15412 Spr. H. Wells D. Coy. G.S.W. left forearm. 9408 Pte. H. Jascoyne C.M.L. G.S.W. right arm. 1754 " Pg. Warburton C. Coy. G.S.W. scalp.	

WAR DIARY / INTELLIGENCE SUMMARY

Army Form C. 2118.

Place	Date	Hour	Summary of Events and Information	Remarks and references to Appendices
Trenches HOUPLINES C11c4.3 to C17c3.2. Sheet 36	1915 6th Nov.		Canbridge Avenue closed for repairs by R.E.	
	7th Nov.		Lt. T.K. Mallett detailed a member of a F.G.C.M. assembled 10 our R.Q.M. Stores, 62 Rue de Lille, Armentières. No 20142 Serjt Gripst "A" Coy. accidentally drowned in Lock East side of River Lys. Whilst crossing narrow bridge sides of lock at HOUPLINES (C.21.c.3.9¾ sheet 36.) He fell off bridge. One officer Major C.E. Porter and 2 min. No. 8 Graham, 9th D.L.I. and No 1116 Pte Green, R.A.M.C. attached 1/5th R. Irish R. unsuccessfully attempted to find him by going into the water. The lock was dragged before the body could be recovered. Casualty:- No 21/442 Pte. Cunningham R. "A" Coy 6 S.W. Coy. forearm.	
"	8th Nov.		4 Platoons 8th Lincolns attached for trench instruction. F.G.C.M. assembled at our headquarters at 2.30 p.m.	
	9th Nov.		8th D.L.I. relieved battalion in trenches. 9.30 a.m. Boys killed in village HOUPLINES.	
	10th Nov.		Battalion left village HOUPLINES about 11.45 a.m. resting in ARMENTIÈRES for 2 an hour, during half men partook of hurried ration. Bn. left ARMENTIÈRES about 1-15 p.m. and marched to Rest Fields (Fields A.9.8.14.15+ sheet 36) about 2 miles WEST of STEENWERCK station, arriving at our destination about 4 p.m. Strength marching out 26 officers, 718 other ranks. Men billeted in farms etc. Men to bed killed by 8 p.m. daily. Lights out 8.30 p.m.	

Army Form C. 2118.

WAR DIARY
or
INTELLIGENCE SUMMARY.
(Erase heading not required.)

Instructions regarding War Diaries and Intelligence Summaries are contained in F.S. Regs., Part II. and the Staff Manual respectively. Title pages will be prepared in manuscript.

Place	Date	Hour	Summary of Events and Information	Remarks and references to Appendices
STEENWERCKE	19/1/15			
(part of)	Nov 8,9,10,11,14,15+14		Battalion rested. Passes to BAILLEUL and places outside Brigade	
			notarea, granted to 50% of officers and 25% of other ranks. This	
		11th Nov.	ratio to continue until 14th Nov.	
	12th Nov.		Battalion Dry Canteen opened at the Estaminet "La Blanche	
			Maison". Canteen to be open between hours of 2 to 5 p.m. daily.	
	13th Nov.		All roads in area flooded. At some parts under water to depth of	
			a depth of 18". Outdoor training impossible. Draft of 25	
			other ranks joined Battalion from No 4 Entrenching Battalion.	
"	14th Nov.		Frost. Frost nearly disappeared. Roads passable nearly all	
			parts of area.	
"	15th Nov.		Armourer Sergeant commenced a thorough inspection of	
			rifles of battalion. Floods gone and training as per	
			programme commenced. Major Denny proceeded on her	
			Major Potter took over command of Battalion.	
	16th Nov.		Lt. Col. Heath rejoined from England and took over	
			command of battalion.	
	19th Nov.		No men sent to BAILLEUL for baths as an arrangement as water	
			supply failed.	
	20th Nov.		Capt. P. A. Read member of A.V. Corps assembled our 1st Btn	
		10 a.m.	Lt. Dickinson attended foundation.	

Army Form C. 2118.

WAR DIARY
INTELLIGENCE SUMMARY.
(Erase heading not required.)

Instructions regarding War Diaries and Intelligence Summaries are contained in F. S. Regs., Part II. and the Staff Manual respectively. Title pages will be prepared in manuscript.

Place	Date	Hour	Summary of Events and Information	Remarks and references to Appendices
STEENWERCKE Part of J.8, N.15 & 14. J.N.13.36.	1915 22nd Nov.		Battalion and 1st Line Transport marched past Army Commander General Plumer - Appx 8.1 - Appx 28 - about 10.15 am. 2/Lt. A. Dickson & 2/Lt. "C" Coy. proceeded to ZUYTPEENE, to attend course of instruction at N.C.O. school. 2523 6/Pte Hodgson proceeded to TENDESHEM school for course of instruction in Grenades.	
	23rd Nov.		60 men per Coy. and a proportion of details attended a gas (chlorine) demonstration. Parties marched through trench filled with gas for about 30 yards.	
	26th Nov.		2/Lt. Hargreaves with 4 men per Coy. and also 1 officer from each Coy. attended lecture on "Intelligence" at CAISSE DE PRAGUE RUE DE COISSONS, BAILLEUL.	
	27th Nov.		No 2382 L/Cpl Marsden proceeded to WISQUES for a course of Instruction on the Machine Gun. Major E.W. Haslam proceeded to England.	
	30th Nov.		Major Darby proceeded to OUTERSTEENE to take over temporary command of 5th Bn. D.L.I. 150th Bde. Major Potter took over Majority. No 1290 Pte J.C. Wyckerley and 1729 Pte E. Hollingworth D. Coy. proceeded to CAESTRE to join 182 Tunnelling Co. R.E.	

WRO⟶ am major

Capt. 1/5th N. Lanc. Regt.

151st Inf.Bde.
50th Div.

Battn. attached to
26th Inf.Bde. 9th
Div. 21.12.15.

(Note: This Battn.
joined 166th Inf.
Bde. (55th Div.)
upon formation of
latter January 1916).

1/5th BATTN. THE LOYAL NORTH LANCASHIRE REGIMENT.

D E C E M B E R

1 9 1 5

1/5th Bn. Loyal N. Lancs. Regt.

Army Form C. 2118.

WAR DIARY
or
INTELLIGENCE SUMMARY.
(Erase heading not required.)

Place	Date	Hour	Summary of Events and Information	Remarks and references to Appendices
STEENWERCK. Sh.Co of A,7,8,14,15, + H. Sheet 36.	1/12/15		N? 2536 L/Sgt. L.Langrish, B. Coy + N? 2510 L/Cpl. R. Bayley C.Coy. proceeded to Cadre School at BLENDECQUES for course of instruction. Working party of 250 other ranks to report at 62 LA CRECHE at 9 a.m. this party to be furnished daily. Battalion billets in billets.	
	2/12/15		Notified by Brigade that we must be prepared to join next Division (65th - West Lancs.) soon, upon joining 2nd Army are. Sgt. Major Awards. Col. Grathyn, Sgt. Laverey Pl.? Whitehead Col. Farnworth, + Cpl. Gledhill interviewed by Brigadier re applications for Commissions.	
	3/12/15		N? 2198 Pte. O.S. Hughes A Coy attached to A.D.T.S. II Corps for period of Christmas pressure.	
	4/12/15		Battalion cross country race run in afternoon. Start 2.15 p.m. Course - twice round billeting area via sundry ditches and other natural obstacles. Winner - N? 2382 Pte. A. Litchfield. Winning team: N? 16 Talbot. A Coy. 85 runners completed the course. 80 runners were officially accounted for. Very warm all over the area.	
	5/12/15		Billeting area still flooded. Brig. Genl. then presented prizes and congratulations to winners of cross country race. Notification from Brigade re increased allotment for leave. Men were able to produce on leave from 6th to 10th inclusive. Pay and from 11th inclusive increased to 3/6 per day.	

1/5th Royal W. Lanc. Rgt.

Army Form C. 2118.

WAR DIARY
or
INTELLIGENCE SUMMARY.
(Erase heading not required.)

Instructions regarding War Diaries and Intelligence Summaries are contained in F.S. Regs., Part II and the Staff Manual respectively. Title pages will be prepared in manuscript.

Place	Date	Hour	Summary of Events and Information	Remarks and references to Appendices
Billets Steenwerck Factory A.Q.8. Sh.14. Sheet 36	7th Dec 15		Major N.R.H. Danne rejoined Battalion. Major F.A.O. Read - Pidcock & Cont. of Infantry assembled at 6. D. Z. I. sh.Q.no 3.30.p.m.	
	9th Dec. 15		Major W.H. Potter detailed as President of F.G.C.M assembled at our H.Q.	
	10th Dec 15		First batch of 33 men proceeded on leave. Reserve formed. Almost all roads in billeting area completely under water.	
	11th Dec 15			
	12th Dec. 15		No 1036 Pte. M. Davies I Coy. accidentally drowned in floods, whilst returning from Steenwerck station off leave. He with Cpl. Smith & two other men also 1st Infantry escape managed to get out of the water. The party were returning to their Billets in a Maltese cart in the early morning - about 2 am. - and the darkness which was intense, the cart ran over a little off the track of the road road into a stream at A 11.d.5.5. Sh.14.36. Meters flooded road submerged and horse was drowned. Pte No 10 Pte Westly submerged and party at the occurrence. Brigade identified Sym Pathy at the occurrence.	
	13th Dec. 15		Major G.H. Potter went on Instructional Course at II Army Area.	
	14th Dec 15		Pte Hargraves 4th Scouts proceeded to W.L.&SW fir Instruction of telescopic sight. Instruction reach N.O. for F.Newell inspection & address by Corps on Brigade members	

1/5th John Lanc Regt

Army Form C. 2118.

WAR DIARY
or
INTELLIGENCE SUMMARY.
(Erase heading not required.)

Instructions regarding War Diaries and Intelligence Summaries are contained in F.S. Regs., Part II. and the Staff Manual respectively. Title pages will be prepared in manuscript.

Place	Date	Hour	Summary of Events and Information	Remarks and references to Appendices
Billets	5th-17th Dec.		Major J.R. Smith who proceeded to England took part to W.O. & trip to R.E.	
Port of Ax — March Aux 30.			By train & aft. 2 min proceeded to WIZERNE for two rounds	
16th Dec.	16		of clothes & twenty nights.	
17th Dec.			Furnished guard at Baths 11-4-2-7.	
18th Dec.			Major W.R.H. Dean proceeded to take over command of 11th (since Lieut. Col. Cheshire Regt.) 2nd Division.	
			1 O.R. 5th Bn. not in trenches, attached by Brigadier	
			20/10 Pte. No. O'Brien, 1 Coy. proceeded to HAVRE, selected for ammunition work	
19th Dec.	19		German gas attack on 6th Division front at 4.00 G.T. no succeed recorded.	
21st Dec.	19		Clothing for regiment of 50th Division limitated	
			Battalion left 3/19 & 5/19 and 60th Division attached to 10 Corps	
			to 20th Infy Brig. 1 Do O'Brien to report for loying brick at CASSEL	
			Lift had to be hurried with until 25th	
22nd Dec.	19		9th Div. attack no two leave vacancies daily pending	
			unallocated by II Corps	
23rd Dec.	16		Major Bower proceeded to England on official leave	
25th Dec.	19		Xmas day. No training no hurried messages of greeting received from decisively the King, Lord Derby, Major Genl. Hogge, Lieut. Colonel Jilliam, 29th W. Lanc. — Lt. Col. Jno Slater. Asst.D.N. Lancs &c	

2353 Wt. W2544/1454 700,000 5/15 D. D. & L. A.D.S.S./Forms/C. 2118.

Army Form C. 2118.

1/5th Bn L'cash. Lancs. Rgt

WAR DIARY
or
INTELLIGENCE SUMMARY.
(Erase heading not required.)

Place	Date	Hour	Summary of Events and Information	Remarks and references to Appendices
Sulluja S.W.E Nordheim Redoubt A.9.B.mh.32.5/4.M	30 Dec. 1916		Commencement of Platoon Competitions in the following subjects:- (1) Bomb throwing - one yard. (2) Platoon drill. (3) Turn out by at C.O's. (4) Bomb Try at C.O's. (5) Wearing of equipment (6) Field work in trenches Judges: the C.O. 2nd in Comd. Umpires: Serjt. Major A Watts.	

M Haskett Pritt
Comdg 1/5 L.N.L Rgt

www.ingramcontent.com/pod-product-compliance
Lightning Source LLC
Chambersburg PA
CBHW081441160426
43193CB00013B/2350